The Early Development of Mohammedanism

David S. Margoliouth

Simon Publications, Inc.
2003

Library of Congress Control Number: 14014594

ISBN: 1-931541-94-9

Published by Simon Publications, Inc. P. O. Box 321, Safety Harbor, FL 34695

THE HIBBERT LECTURES
SECOND SERIES
1913

THE HIBBERT LECTURES
SECOND SERIES

THE
EARLY DEVELOPMENT
OF MOHAMMEDANISM

LECTURES
DELIVERED IN THE UNIVERSITY OF LONDON
MAY AND JUNE 1913

BY

D. S. MARGOLIOUTH, D.Litt.

FELLOW OF NEW COLLEGE AND LAUDIAN PROFESSOR OF ARABIC IN THE
UNIVERSITY OF OXFORD

LONDON
WILLIAMS AND NORGATE
14 HENRIETTA STREET, COVENT GARDEN, W.C.
1914

PREFACE

THE following lectures were delivered in the months
of May and June 1913, in the University of London,
at the request of the HIBBERT TRUSTEES, to whom
the writer wishes at the outset to express his cordial
thanks, both for selecting the subject of Mohammedanism and committing the treatment of it to him.
Professor Goldziher in his *Lectures on Islam*[1] has
provided guidance for all who wish to handle this
theme; the topic chosen by the present writer might
be called "the supplementing of the Koran," *i.e.* the
process whereby the *ex tempore*, or indeed *ex momento*,
utterances thrown together in that volume were
worked into a fabric which has marvellously resisted
the ravages of time.

The materials employed for these lectures are to
a small extent unpublished MSS.,[2] but in the main
recently published works of early Islamic authors.
Of three among the most eminent of these the
writer is simultaneously publishing for the first time

---

[1] *Vorlesungen über den Islam,* Heidelberg, 1910.

[2] The chief of these are the works of Muḥāsibī, employed in
Lecture V.; the *Mawāḳif* of Niffarī, from which select translations
are given in Lecture VI.; and the monograph of Ibn 'Asākir on
Abu'l-Ḥasan al-Ash'arī, which has been used for Lecture VII.

authentic and copious biographies from a MS. in his possession, through the liberality of the GIBB TRUSTEES.[1] The works of one of them, the jurist Shāfiʿī, were printed by Cairene scholars in the years 1903–1907; the light which they throw on the history of Islamic jurisprudence is brilliant. Their publication was immediately preceded by that of the works ascribed to Shāfiʿī's teacher Mālik, himself the founder of a law-school; and these, too, are of the greatest utility. This year has seen the completion of a *Corpus Juris* on a still vaster scale belonging to the school of Abū Ḥanīfah, but compiled three centuries after his time; this, though highly instructive, is no substitute for the work of the founder. The biography of Shāfiʿī certainly helps the appreciation and possibly the understanding of his treatises.

Of the other two authors, Jāḥiẓ and Ṭabarī, the works have been issued partly by Eastern, partly by Western scholars. Each of these is a mine of information, and, like Shāfiʿī, takes us into the atmosphere wherein Islam developed.

In Lecture IV., which deals with the condition of the "protected communities," considerable use has been made of later authorities; elsewhere the writer has usually endeavoured to keep within the third, with occasional extension into the fourth, Islamic century. M. Massignon's interesting edition of a work by Ḥallāj enables us to follow Ṣūfism into a period near its rise; the account of this

---

[1] Yāḳūt's *Dictionary of Learned Men*, vol. vi.

subject given in Lecture V. is mainly based on the *Ḳūt al-Ḳulūb* of Abū Ṭālib al-Mekkī, of the middle fourth century of Islam, published some twenty years ago. Lecture VII. contains material drawn from the *Ibānah*, ascribed to Abu'l-Ḥasan al-Ashʿarī, of which the genuineness seems to be attested by Ibn ʿAsākir; it was printed some ten years ago in Hyderabad. Another text printed in the same place, the *Dalāʾil al-Nubuwwah* of ʿAbū Nuʿaim, has furnished material for Lecture VIII.

Throughout, an acquaintance with the elements of the subject, such as can be obtained from the writer's manuals,[1] has been assumed in the reader; in order, however, to render the Lectures intelligible by themselves, all allusions which could occasion any difficulty have been explained in the Index.

The writer terminates this Preface with a tribute of gratitude to those Mohammedan scholars in Egypt and India who during the last few years have put into our hands so many texts of the highest importance for the study of Arabic antiquity; and another to the audiences who deemed these lectures worthy of their attention.

OXFORD, *December* 1913.

---

[1] *Mohammedanism*, in the "Home University Library," and *Mohammed and the Rise of Islam* in the series "Heroes of the Nations."

CONTENTS

THE
EARLY DEVELOPMENT
OF MOHAMMEDANISM

LECTURE I

THE KORAN AS THE BASIS OF ISLAM

IT is a noteworthy fact about the Mohammedan system that since the Migration it has demanded no qualifications for admission to its brotherhood. To those who are outside its pale it in theory offers no facilities whatever for the study of its nature ; a man must enroll himself as a member first, and then only may he learn what his obligations are. The Koran may not be sold to Unbelievers ; soldiers are advised not to take it with them into hostile territory for fear the Unbeliever should get hold of it ; and many a copy bears upon it a warning to Unbelievers not to touch. Pious grammarians have refused to teach grammar to Jews or Christians, because the rules were apt to be illustrated by quotations from the sacred volume. The Unbeliever is by one of the codes [1] forbidden to enter a mosque ; and even when

---

[1] Mālik. *See* Baiḍāwī i. 10, 12.

1

1

permission is granted him to do so, he is an unwelcome guest.   The crowning ceremony of Islam, the Pilgrimage, may be witnessed by no Unbeliever; the penalty for intrusion is death.

It follows that such periods of instruction and probation as are enjoined by some other systems upon neophytes are unknown to Islam; and indeed there is no occasion for them.   Their purpose is to test the neophyte's sincerity in the first place, and his moral worthiness in the second.   Against insincerity the system is sufficiently armed by the principle that whosoever abandons Islam forfeits his life; there is then little danger of men joining for some dishonest purpose and quitting the community when that purpose has been served.   A Moslem who is in peril of his life may indeed simulate perversion, and no difficulty is made about readmitting the repentant pervert; but where Islam can be safely professed the pervert cannot legally hope to be spared.   And it follows from this principle that martyrdom in Islam means something very different from what it means to the Christian.   The Christian martyr is the man who dies professing his faith, but not resisting; the Moslem martyr is one who dies for his faith on the battle-field; more often in endeavouring to force it upon others than defending his own exercise thereof. For his sacred book expressly permits him to refrain from confessing where confession will result in death or torment.

On the other hand, the maxim that Islam cancels all that was before it renders moral qualification unnecessary. Only after the man has joined the community do his acts begin to count. Whatever he may have done before joining may bear some analogy to the keeping or to the breaking of a commandment ; but it is not the same thing. Unbelievers on the Day of Judgment are to be asked two questions only : why they associated other beings with the Almighty, and if Apostles were sent them why they repudiated them. The only thing that is incumbent upon them, the only duty wherewith God has charged them, is to study the evidence of Islam ;[1] or let us rather say, to accept Islam, since they have no access to the evidences. They may by their good qualities win the friendship or even the affection of Moslems, but they are destined to Hell-Fire notwithstanding. An author of the third century A.H., who quotes verses in praise of Jews, Christians, and Mazdians, shows that even encomiasts make no concealment of this fact.[2] A Jewish or Christian physician may be useful to a Moslem, but is none the less the enemy of Allah.

It follows, then, that Islam has to be preached with the sword, for without going into the water one cannot learn to swim, and there is no probationary dip. If the convincing miracle of Islam be the Koran, which outdoes all other compositions in eloquence, the persons who are to be convinced by this miracle must have the opportunity of studying it in order to be convinced. This is so obvious that

---

[1] Al-Farḳ, p. 107.
[2] Jāḥiẓ, Ḥayawān v. 52.

some jurists are inclined to make an exception in favour of a few texts, sufficient to give the inquirer a notion of its contents; and they can quote the precedent of the Prophet, who in his imperious message to all peoples, nations, and languages, commanding them to adopt Islam if they wished for safety, introduced a text from the sacred volume. It is clear, however, that the same objection must really apply to one text as to a number; it would be impossible to fix a limit at which the volume became esoteric. No, let people pay homage to it first, recognise that it is the divine revelation, and then they may, or indeed must, study it. But such recognition can only be extorted by force, if the right to examine is denied. And if methods are to be judged by their results, no one with Mohammed's experience would have regarded argument as an expedient for conversion comparable with the sword. He argued for thirteen years and made converts by the unit or the decade; he drew the sword and won them by the hundred and the thousand. Twenty years of fighting effected more than a thousand years of pleading and arguing would effect. But just as the argument of reason is apt to be weakened if the sword be behind it, so the argument of the sword is not strengthened by the fact that the other form of reasoning has been tried in vain. Hence the periods of inquiry and probation are not desirable.

Now this peculiarity of Islam is closely connected with the history of the system. In the first place, it began as a secret society, and even now, if novelists may be believed, the secret society has a tendency to work upon the same theory. It cannot live or succeed without a steady accretion of members; on the other hand, its purposes can only be communicated to the loyal. It is therefore necessary that members should be committed to the programme of the society before they know what it is.

In the second place, the claim of Mohammed, though he may have formulated it differently at different times, was to be the channel whereby the Almighty communicated His behests to mankind, or at least to some of the Arabs. The two articles of the Moslem faith are reciprocally involved: unless Allah were the sole ruler of the community, the importance attaching to His messenger would be smaller; the importance of the messenger of Allah is a corollary of the unity of Allah. Allah issues orders through the Prophet; that is the meaning of the Islamic creed. Those orders may concern ritual or conduct or politics; and from the nature of human life, with fresh questions ever arising, those orders are likely to be occasional; whence the title " occasions of revelation," given to works which deal with the chronology of the Koran, accurately expresses its nature.

It is this fact which explains and even excuses the carelessness with regard to the Koran which is historically attested of both the Prophet and his Companions. " When the Prophet died," we are told by a preacher, " he left twenty thousand Companions who had not done more than glance at the Koran, and only six who knew the whole by heart—two of these being doubtful cases." " A Companion of the Prophet who knew by heart a long Surah, or a seventh of the Koran, counted as a marvel." It would be truer to say that there was scarcely a Companion of the Prophet who would even have claimed to know the whole by heart: for when the Prophet died it was still in a state of flux. This fact is most easily explained if we suppose the Koran to have been ultimately thought of as a series of messages which do not together constitute a book. Both in Hebrew and Arabic the same word signifies " book " and " letter," and considerable confusion results. The " carriers of the Koran " were the people who knew certain portions of it by heart ; according to an early historian they ran some risk of being exterminated in the campaign of Yemamah which followed shortly after the Prophet's death. And there were many different texts. Few followers of the Prophet would have been present on all the occasions when revelations were delivered ; accident would decide whether such as had been revealed during their absence would ever be communicated to them. At a later period, when traditions were committed to memory, they were ordinarily very brief, usually of a single sentence. The normal memory is not fit to hold more. It is conceivable that, as a tradition informs us, there were Believers famous for collecting much of the Koran, *i.e.* many verses ; but before the Prophet's death no one probably even thought he possessed all. Nor, indeed, would the sense of the word " all " in such a case be clear ; for at an early period of the revelations the doctrine was enunciated that texts could be erased and others substituted ; and if a text be erased, it clearly ceases to have any further existence ; it might figure in a history of Islam or a biography of the Prophet, but could no longer figure in the sacred volume itself. Yet when the Koran was compiled, those responsible for the undertaking were conscious that parts of the work did abrogate other parts, though they did not think it their duty to decide the category to which any particular text belonged ; in a sense, then, their collection was larger than it should have been, because it contained matter for which something better had been substituted, as well as the substitute. So long as the Prophet lived there could be no complete Koran ; his death completed it. It had then to be collected before its nature could be determined.

If we endeavour to analyse the conception of the Koran as revealed to us in the work itself, we shall find most help in a passage of Surah xxix. 46–49 : " And thus have we sent down unto thee the writing, and those to whom we have given the writing believe therein, and among *these* there are such as believe therein, and none deny our signs save the Unbelievers. Neither usedst thou before it to read any writing nor to trace it with thy right hand ; in that case the mendacious would have suspected. Nay, it is distinct signs in the breasts of those who have been given knowledge, and none deny our signs save the iniquitous.   And they say : why have not signs [*i.e.* miracles] been sent down unto him from his Lord ?   Say : the signs are with God only, and I am but a distinct warner.   Does it not then suffice them that we have sent down unto thee the writing to be read unto them ? "   The author is here arguing against those who demand a sign in the sense of *miracle*; he declares that the miracle of the Koran is sufficient.   The practice with regard to books was that one who wished for a copy went to the author and obtained leave to copy the original, or else to hear the author dictating it.   So in the case of a great commentary on the Koran to be mentioned later, the possessor of a copy said he had attended the author's dictation of it for eight years.[1] This theory was current not only in Arabia.   Plato makes Zeno bring his work to Athens and read it aloud.   With the Arabs the custom also prevailed of getting the author to testify to the correctness of the copy.   And the writer of a popular book had to suffer for his success ; Ḥarīrī, the author of the work which perhaps comes second to the Koran in popularity, informs us that he would have introduced a correction had it not been that he had certified seven hundred copies—in the possession of readers who came to him for authorisation—and all these contained the reading which he would gladly have changed.   In Mohammed's case the trouble of reading or taking down was spared ; in Surah xxvi. 193 the revelation is brought down to his heart by

1 Yāḳūt vi. 424.

the faithful Spirit, while at the same time it is in the tablets of the ancients. In Surah xxviii. 86 he is told that he had never hoped that the writing would be flung to him. The Unbelievers suggest (vi. 7) that it should have been flung down on parchment so that they could touch it with their hands; they are told that they would have regarded such procedure as imposture or legerdemain. On the other hand, if they had been allowed to see an angel bringing it down, that angel would have either annihilated them, or else he would have had to appear in human shape, whence the suspicion of imposture could not have been avoided. Still this " writing " is at once in the tablets of the ancients, *i.e.* in the hands of Jews and Christians, and is also miraculously communicated to the Prophet. When this miraculously communicated text is found to agree with the matter contained in the tablets or charts of the monotheists, and for this the evidence of an Israelite is adduced, obviously a miracle has taken place, and Mohammed is divinely authorised to communicate the Book of God.

He communicates it in his own language, but whether the original is in Arabic is not clear ; there is at least a suggestion that it is in a divine language : " We have made it an Arabic Koran that ye might understand it, but in the original with us it is sublime, wise " (xliii. 2). " Sublime, wise " probably means in an exalted and learned language. " Easing it with thy tongue " (xliv. 58) probably means translating it into Arabic. Its name Koran, " reading," refers to the Prophet's own mental experience. The earliest revelation, if we may believe the tradition, is one wherein he is told to read, and indeed what God had taught with the pen ; and in another passage, with reference to this text, God is said to have enjoined upon him the reading (xxviii. 85). To many of the Surahs letters of the alphabet are pre-fixed, ordinarily followed by some such sentence as, T.S.M. " Those are the letters of the perspicuous writing "; A.L.M. " That is the writing, there is no mistaking it "; T.S. " Those are the letters of the reading and a perspicuous writing "; A.L.M. " Those are the letters of the wise writing "; H.M.A.S.Q. " Thus doth God reveal unto thee as unto thy predecessors " — phrases which indicate that these letters are specimens of the original writing which Mohammed translates into Arabic in order to com-municate it to his fellows. The original is in God's possession, and like other authors He can alter His work at pleasure. In the year 67 A.H., one 'Abdallah Ibn Nauf, who delivered oracles in the style of the Koran, prophesied a victory for his party, naming a certain Wednesday ; they were defeated. When taunted with his error, he quoted the maxim of the Koran, " God possesses the original of the Book, and can erase or enter what He likes " (xiii. 39).[1] The prophecy failed to come true because the original of the divine book had been altered. This right of alteration which the author possesses at once explains divergence in the Koran from the contents of earlier revelations, and divergence between the

---

[1] Ṭabarī ii. 732.

matter communicated to the Prophet at different times.

That the contents were not communicated all at once, as is perhaps the case with ordinary books, which may be supposed to be recited continuously, or at least at successive periods, was noticed by Mohammed's contemporaries as a fact requiring explanation; and the accounts given are the convenience of the hearers (xvii. 107), and the confirming of the Prophet's mind (xxv. 34). Possibly the meaning of this latter phrase is " to render the Prophet's grasp of it more certain." Whether these explanations were adequate or not, it was most important that it should not be communicated all at once; for the value of the Koran clearly lay in what it added to former versions of the Scriptures, not in what it shared with them. The reasoning which underlies the Surahs that have been quoted is curiously like that which we employ in the case of MSS. unearthed. We possess fragments of various works known in antiquity; say an ostensible copy of one of these works were produced, we should at once look out for the fragments already known; and one of the tests of its genuineness would be its containing those fragments; only its value would not lie in those fragments, but in what it added to them. Hence the agreement of the Koran with earlier revelations had in the main evidential value, proving that the Prophet had really been chosen to communicate the divine book to his fellows; its intrinsic value lay in what it added to earlier revelations.

At times it claimed to settle points which those revelations had left obscure; at times to alter what they contained, on the principle which we have already seen.

Now, as we have seen, the word used for " book " in Arabic also means " letter," and considerable confusion results. A book is doubtless in all cases a message, but a message is not necessarily a book. The message need be of no permanent importance, having reference to a momentary emergency. Similarly, a messenger—which is the name whereby Mohammed ordinarily describes himself—is thought of as bringing an order or piece of information required for an immediate need rather than as communicating what is to be permanent. The ambassador communicates the wishes of his government as they arise; those wishes are usually no more permanent than the occasions with which they are concerned. And although the Koran is thought of at times as read by the Prophet from the original which he could mentally see, in many cases perhaps the rendering " despatch " would be truer than the rendering " book." It has been noticed that the word which we ordinarily render " reveal," and which literally means " send down," is properly applied to royal rescripts; the suppliant " raises " a petition and the sovereign " sends down " the reply. The faithful at Medinah used to await fresh revelations each day somewhat as we in these days are on the look out for the morning paper. The formula which we not unfrequently find employed, " They will ask thee: say," or " They will say, but say thou," is such as belongs to temporary embarrassment or temporary controversy. The objection or difficulty which has been raised is settled, and it is presumed that it will not recur.

At neither the Meccan nor the Medinese period of the Koranic revelation was its nature such as to give it permanence. In the former period there was constant repetition of the same matter; and the Prophet, reading off the celestial original, naturally repeatedly read the same material. There is, then, some variation in the detail, but little in the general trend of the discourses. The disagreement is not more considerable than that between the three accounts, say, of the conversion of St Paul in the Acts of the Apostles. It is clearly not the intention of the author of that work to give accounts of the same event which supplement one another; still less accounts which contradict each other; his desire is not to repeat himself literally. And the same rhetorical or artistic principle underlies the Koranic treatment of the legends of the Prophets. The tales are told vividly; and this vividness excludes literal repetition. They are, so to speak, repeated presentations of the same theme, not copies printed off the same types. Some of these sermons would be more impressive than others, and occasionally a passage would occur which would attract special attention; but the general sameness of the matter would prevent any discourse being thought to have permanent value, unless, indeed, some passages were selected for use in common worship.

When the Prophet went to Medinah, the Koran assumed another form, but even this was no more likely to secure permanence. It dealt very largely with current events, drawing morals from the immediate past instead of employing for this purpose the mythical or historical past. It explained why the Moslems had been defeated at Uḥud, why the Prophet had taken the wife of his adopted son, why he had evaded a promise made . to his wives ; it defended the honour of ‘Ā’ishah, it extolled various victories, it threatened the hostile and the disaffected. It regulated various forms of procedure, the division of inheritances, the attestation of wills, disputes between married couples, the etiquette of the Prophet's court. The interest attaching to few of these subjects would seem to be permanent ; when the defeat at Uḥud had been wiped out by a signal victory, only antiquarian interest would attach to it, and few would wish to remember the scandal about ‘Ā’ishah. On the other hand, there was no reason why the Prophet should be bound by his own precedents, since he expressly reserved to Allah the right to revise the Koran. Even its legislation, owing to the possibility of its being revised, was scarcely felt to have permanent value ; when the Prophet was asked to decide a case, he had to wait until a revelation dealing with it was vouchsafed him, and. he was not even entitled to specify the time wherein he could count on such a communication being delivered.[1] Since it is rare that two actual

<hr>

[1] Shāfi‘ī, Umm vii. 271.

cases correspond in every detail, it would be better on some later occasion that the Prophet should be similarly favoured than that he should have to depend on the accuracy of his memory or of a document. While, then, the Prophet lived, the Koran could not acquire the importance which it afterwards received, and it is probable that little concern was bestowed on any parts save those regularly used in liturgy.

To accept Islam meant simply to promise obedience to the Prophet, according to some authorities in matters lawful and honourable, but such a stipulation has little meaning when the Prophet was recognised as the dictator in such matters. And where the undertaking given is of this sort, the word "system" is inapplicable; since the dictator cannot say what he may dictate, there is no reason why he should tie his hands. The obligations were not specified because they had not been defined.

Whether the Prophet gave much consideration to the effects of his own death is uncertain; this is, we are told, a matter whereon mankind are most inconsistent. The possibilities of the present dispensation coming to an end and of his own death, which indeed he seems sometimes to think of as an alternative, were clearly considered during the difficulties and stress of the Meccan period; when he became despot of a community he appears to have been too much occupied with other things to pay much attention to such matters. There is a tradition that he prophesied the complete extinction of the race within a hundred years of his time, but its authenticity is denied.[1] A theory that, like the Christian Messiah, he was to return was preached not long after his death, and based on a verse of the Koran, but the preacher seems to have found few adherents;[2] for some reason or other the sects which looked forward to the appearance of a hidden Messiah ordinarily fixed on someone else. The common-sense which Mohammed almost invariably displayed makes us unwilling to suppose that he regarded himself as immune from the common calamity, though we are told that his followers at first declined to believe in his death when it occurred, and that some Arab tribes made this occurrence an excuse for rejecting Islam. There is a story that on his deathbed he desired to dictate a code, but that those who heard him supposed him to be in delirium, and declined to take advantage of this offer. If this be true, it indicates how deeply they were impressed with the belief that the Koran was a divine composition wherein the Prophet him- self had no hand ; for any ostensible revelation would have been welcomed and implicitly obeyed.

Still, like other prophets and legislators, Mohammed, died, and he had made no provision for a successor, or at least any such provision was suppressed. Prophets arose in Arabia, but they were not of this fold, and their claims were rejected unheard by those who had accepted the claims of Mohammed. Of modern critics very few, and of ancient Moslems

[1] Mukhtalif al-Ḥadīth, p. 119.
[2] Ṭabarī i. 2942. Surah xxviii. 85.

scarcely any, put into practice the doctrine of the Koran that one prophet is as good as another: that " we make no distinction between any of them." Yet it might seem that if the claim of any one man to legislate and govern by inspiration be admitted, we are not entitled to reject unheard that of another. If there be any uniformity in the conduct of the world, it is difficult to think of any one age being so favoured as to have the living presence of a divine ambassador, while previous and subsequent ages must content themselves with a prospect and a retrospect. Nevertheless, this is what the Moslem system assumes; the place of the Prophet is occupied by a prince, a deputy, authorised to conduct the affairs of the community, but by no means either in direct communication with the Deity or empowered to tamper with the rulings of the Prophet. Among those who enjoyed power during the first century of Islam perhaps the adventurer Mukhtār, who was for a short time supreme in Kufah, was the only pretender to mysterious powers. He claimed to be infallible,[1] and conveyed his commands in a style closely modelled on that of the Koran. His prayers were regarded by his lieutenants as the best of reinforcements.[2] When called " Liar," he pointed out that other " Prophets " had been similarly designated. He established a cult of a Sacred Chair which was something between a Urim and Thummim and an Ark of the Covenant.[3] Nevertheless, he

---

[1] Ṭabarī ii. 626.   [2] *Ibid.*, 644, 13.
[3] *Ibid.*, 706.

claimed to be acting not on his own account, but on that of the Mahdī, *i.e.* the divinely guided member of the Prophet's household, who seems to have been somewhat shy of acknowledging this agent. And, indeed, a theory arose that the Prophet's family were the true interpreters of the Koran, possessed of mysterious knowledge, which prevented them from making mistakes. In the latest period of the Umayyad dynasty, while the two branches of the Prophet's house were still united in a common aim, a preacher not only states this doctrine, but declares that all the adherents of the Prophet's house were agreed about it. An agent who came with proper credentials from the head of the family must be a competent agent; the danger that Satan might have misled the head of the family in his interpretation of the Koran need not even be considered.[1] A few years before this we are told that the adherents of the Prophet's family attributed to them knowledge of futurity, and even made them objects of worship.[2] And this doctrine was never abandoned by the Prophet's descendants and their adherents, but it was not adopted for any practical purpose by the heirs of his uncle, who for the most important period of Islam were supreme.

Had the claims been accepted of one of those prophets who arose after Mohammed's death, a state of affairs analogous to what existed when he was at Medinah would for a time have continued; the nearest possible approach to a theocracy, since the

---

[1] Ṭabarī ii. 1961.   [2] *Ibid.*, 1682.

community would always have been subject to an accredited representative of its god: bound by no code and attached to no precedents. The rejection of these claims closed the avenue to the divine communications, whereon the community could no longer rely for guidance. To have accepted the claim of one or other of these prophets would have necessitated another break with the past, for this whole theory of prophets implies that the operation of the Divine Being in the world is spasmodic, not continuous; there would have been no guarantee that the system elaborated by Mohammed during a decade of years might not be violently upset. Moreover, though the Creed recognised him only, the Refugees and Helpers had played a conspicuous part in his career; if they would not have come into existence without him, he would have failed egregiously without them. For a time, then, in spite of his removal, the organisation which he had created could continue.

According to all appearances the death of the Prophet made at first little difference in the conduct of affairs, because his successors were his most trusted advisers, the persons most familiar with his ideas and plans. And the extraordinary series of successes which occupied these years rendered the cessation of prophecy easily tolerable; for the most frequent purpose of prophecy in the years at Medinah had been apology and polemic, for neither of which was there now any occasion. That the Prophet's household should have been unable to form a dangerous party within the state is certainly remarkable; that they were not able to do this must be explained partly by the political incompetence of Ali, which afterwards became notorious, partly by the fact that his relations with the Prophet's daughter, his wife, were wanting in cordiality. Hence the Companions were able to thrust the Prophet's family aside, and even deprive them of their inheritance, without endangering the permanence of the state which he had founded. And it is possible that the maxim whereby this procedure was justified was put into the Prophet's mouth, made one of his Acta, by them.

These Acta, however, no one thought of collecting and preserving, and though the Prophet's letters had the force of law in his lifetime, there was no one who performed the service which has been so useful to posterity in the case of the correspondence of Cicero or of St Paul. Probably there must be some literary tradition current in a community before the desirability of such procedure occurs; and such literary tradition was wanting in both Meccah and Medinah, nor could that of the more civilised nations speedily to be subdued be assimilated before some decades had elapsed. The scribes who had composed the Prophet's letters and the persons to whom they had been delivered were not conscious of their historic importance. And, as has already been seen, their appreciation of the despatches from Almighty God was not much more intense. Doubtless, some verses of these despatches had to be recited in the daily worship, but according to some authorities it was of no consequence which the verses were; provided they formed part of the Koran, any which the worshipper remembered might be repeated by him in his orisons.[1] The importance of the sacred book grew at first slowly, though with accelerating pace; but the consequences of the original neglect can be found in the earliest and best of the commentaries. Where we expect certainty, we find guesswork and fiction. Even the two recensions of the Koran are confused by the great Ṭabari.[2] There are allusions to which the key is lost, though we should have expected that anyone who was in Medinah when the verses were first recited would have been able to explain them. If the commentaries on the Koran be compared with, say, the Greek comments on Homer, which do not claim to be more than the guesses of a later age on the sense of an ancient text, the difference is scarcely noticeable. The certainty which belongs to an authoritative tradition is wanting in both cases.

Both indulge constantly in what might be called cheap fictions—stories intended to account for the verses such as anyone could invent, and which, therefore, have nothing convincing about them. Even where explanations which we know from some other source to be true are given, side by side with them false comments are recorded as of equal authority. Nor do correct explanations give the appearance of being handed down by persons who

___

[1] Shāfi'ī, Umm i. 88.   [2] Comm. iii. 24.

experienced the original delivery of the messages, but rather of being the result of conscious and erudite combination. And this indicates that the value assigned to the revelations by their contemporaries was quite different from that which is assigned to a permanent code. The revelations were thought of as solutions of questions that cropped up, modes of dealing with difficulties, or as having reference to particular emergencies, particular states of mind experienced by the Prophet or his followers, or even his enemies. However great the anxiety which these may have occasioned at the time, those eventful years speedily brought other experiences which obscured the former; the crises were too numerous for excessive importance to be attached to any. And, in any case, the crisis was more likely to be remembered than the revelation associated with it. So long as the Prophet was among them the living voice was vastly more important than the letters which had been recited and largely served their purpose. The persons who knew may never have been asked about the import of particular words and phrases, and had no occasion to communicate their knowledge; no systematic teaching had begun before the best authorities had passed away. And we have, besides, to take account of the fact that at times it may not have been thought desirable to communicate the truth.

No contradiction should ever surprise us in human conduct, and there are numerous analogies which help us to understand the attitude of the early

Moslems towards the words of their Prophet and their God. " This man spake as never man spake " —that is recorded of the Founder of Christianity ; yet, in spite of Christian dogma, we are still relegated to the region of conjecture as to the language in which these discourses were delivered, and the persons who are responsible for the translations in which we possess them. In the case of the Koran we are at least in possession of certainty with regard to these two points : the language and the collectors. And though, as shall be seen, great importance was not attached by the earliest Moslems to the wording of the Koran, still it was known to embody an artifice which secured a certain amount, though only a limited amount, of permanence, and which distinguished the matter composing it from any that was not intentionally fabricated so as to resemble it. Texts which had formed part of the divine revelation were known to be cast in a certain mould ; and although that mould was somewhat elastic, the restriction on possible revelations which resulted was considerable. Verse compositions were excluded, for the Prophet had not been taught versification ; prose compositions were excluded because the genuine verses had an artifice, though one, it is true, of extreme simplicity. Further, we find in the Koran itself the dogma that the style of the book is inimitable, and those who believed the Prophet accepted the dogma, and in a way perhaps expected that the Koran could take care of itself. In general, however, we attribute the carelessness with regard to this possession to want of familiarity with literary methods and habits.

But a vision gains in importance by being sealed, and more than once in the Jewish and Christian Scriptures do we come across a command to seal the book, meaning not to secrete its contents, but to terminate it definitely so as to exclude the possibility of further additions. The liability to abrogation, the ephemeral and occasional nature of the revelations which prevented their hearers from overestimating their value, disappeared when once the spring of revelation had run dry. The book may have been closed more than once in the Prophet's time, just as he may have received more than one command to contract no more marriages; but so long as a man lives he can change his mind; God could alter the text. After the removal of the Prophet the messages which he had delivered could take his place to some extent, as being an authority which no one dare question. The consternation of the Moslems at the death of the Prophet was, according to the tradition, allayed by a quotation from the Koran wherein the Prophet's death was foretold; that quotation appears then to have been heard for the first time. The lessons impressed on the mind of the person who produced this text may well have been two: the value of the Koran to those who possessed it, and the danger of leaving this possession unguarded. Short as was the reign of the first successor, barely two years, and those occupied by campaigns, the need for a collection of the Koran became acutely felt, and an order was issued for its execution.   The prophecy had to be sealed.   And the first successor, having followed the Prophet from the commencement of his career, and been his inseparable companion, would be likely to know better than anyone else what had or had not been revealed.

Although the traditions which are quoted in connection with this scheme must be received with caution, they seem rightly to represent the difficulty as appalling.   Our best authority does not appear to countenance the supposition that any part of the Koran was in writing; for had it existed in that state, the danger that it would perish with the death of the Islamic champions would not have been serious. In the first account of Ṭabarī it is the collector who first writes it on the naïve materials at his disposal ; the second successor of the Prophet has it transferred from these to a scroll, which remained in the possession of his daughter, but was afterwards " washed out " by order of the third successor.   In the Koran itself there is a reference to Scripture-Readers, persons besides the Prophet who read aloud the texts (xxii. 71) ; it is likely that these men would have committed them to memory from MS., although they found permanent lodging in their breasts. Indeed, the difficulty of teaching without the use of writing is so great that we can scarcely believe any lengthy document would be committed to memory any other way.   When, however, the texts had been thoroughly learned, the leaflet which had been employed in the process of learning would have no further value and might be allowed to perish. And so the mockers are thought of as "hearing and knowing," not as possessing and reading (xlv. 7, 8).

The collector is represented as consulting all the Meccan and Medinese followers of the Prophet, and putting down what they had "got," *i.e.* such texts as they had learned; his main difficulty must have lain in the fact already noticed—that the Surahs were largely repetition of the same matter, with at times slight, at other times considerable, variations. A preacher or lecturer may well have occasion to repeat the same statements or their substance a great number of times; but such repetition has no place in a book, wherein the same text can be repeatedly read, least of all in a communication from Almighty God. The theory that precepts may be occasional, *i.e.* vary with different circumstances, is admissible; but the opinion of the Divine Being on ancient history cannot possibly vary. Where on one occasion the Koran quotes a number of different opinions about a difficult matter, viz. the number of the Sleepers in the Cave and whether their dog counted or not, it is to condemn them all as conjectures, not to record them as possible solutions. Hence the collector had to settle the difficult question whether he should treat each separate account of the story of Moses or Abraham as a distinct Surah, or whether they should be regarded as different versions of the same. There is a tradition that the Prophet, when discrepancies in reading were called to his attention and he had declared all readings correct, explained that the Koran had been revealed in seven texts; which may mean that the same passage in the original Koran had been reproduced by him in seven different ways. Probably the Prophet, had the scheme of collecting the Koran come into his mind, would have selected one version of each story and abrogated the others; but to do this certainly exceeded the power of anyone but himself.

It is usual to suppose that the last or ultimate version in such a case is the best and most authoritative; and though ordinarily the different versions of the same narrative make no reference to each other, sometimes the mode of statement gives an impression of being a corrected edition or an increased edition of what has preceded. So in the lengthy account of Pharaoh and Moses in Surah xxviii. we have at the commencement the explanation that Pharaoh divided his people into castes, of which the oppressed, *i.e.* the Israelites, formed one; in Surah xl., besides the ascription to Pharaoh of the desire to build the tower (probably of Babel), a wholly new personage is introduced, viz. a member of the Pharaonic family who believed but concealed his faith, yet nevertheless delivered a homily quite indistinguishable from those customary in the mouths of monotheistic prophets. In Surah xi. the story of Noah is enriched with an account of a son of Noah who disobeyed his father and perished in the Flood. The text observes that this is a mystery which neither the Prophet nor his people had previously known. We should infer that these new details of the story of Noah were what had been unknown before this particular revelation, some account of the patriarch having previously been communicated.

It is not possible for us to locate these Surahs chronologically on the supposition that the accounts gradually grow more to correspond with the Biblical tradition, for the human mind is both receptive and forgetful; the introduction of Haman and Korah into the story of Moses and Pharaoh may be due to access of knowledge, or their omission may be due to such access; this is not a matter whereon we can pronounce *a priori*. The collector may possibly have been able to pursue investigations into the dates of revelation, but where the dating of events was vague, it would be difficult to obtain any accurate information on this subject. Probably, then, he introduced into his collection any copies that he could find of revelations certified to have been actually delivered. And although the repetition is intolerable in the book, it is probable that accurate reporting of the Prophet's discourses during his career of twenty-three years would not have resulted in a much larger volume than the collector put together.

From the fluid nature of the revelation it comes that though the Koran constantly eulogises itself, it rarely quotes itself; the cases in which it takes account of earlier statements are exceptional. A quite exceptional case of a series of references is to be found in connection with the story of Abraham. In Surah xix. 48, which is early in the Meccan period, Abraham promises to ask forgiveness for his father.

In Surah xxvi. 86 he actually does this. He prays, "Forgive my father: he is one of those that go astray." In Surah xiv. 42 he says, "Forgive me and my parents and the Believers on the day whereon the reckoning shall be made," rather implying that Abraham's father was not an Unbeliever. But in Surah ix., nearly at the end of the Prophet's career, verse 114 declares that neither the Prophet nor the Believers have any business to ask forgiveness for the pagans, even though they were their relatives, when it has become clear that they are to be damned; they are thus forbidden to do what Abraham clearly did in Surah xxvi. Hence Surah ix. proceeds: "Now Abraham's praying that his father should be forgiven was only due to a promise which he had made him"; i.e. the promise recorded in Surah xix. is the explanation of Abraham's conduct as recorded in Surah xxvi. And in Surah lx. Abraham's conduct is held up as exemplary, when he and his companions said to their people "We are quit of you and what ye worship other than God; eternal enmity and hatred show themselves between us until ye believe in God only: except the saying of Abraham to his father, 'I will ask forgiveness for thee.'" That, it is allowed, is not to be imitated: it can only be excused. Surah ix. proceeds, in verse 115, "Now when it became clear to Abraham that his father was an enemy to Allah, he declared himself quit of him."

What is clear is that Surahs ix. and lx. recognise the existence of Surahs xix. and xxvi., and it is fairly clear that Surah ix. recognises and appeals to Surah lx.

Equally exceptional are the cases in which we have the contents of two editions side by side. The clearest is perhaps in Surah viii., where verse 66 asserts that one Moslem in war is equal to ten Unbelievers, and this is followed by verse 67, " Now God has lightened the burden upon you, knowing that there is weakness in you," and reduced the proportion by eighty per cent. ; one Believer is to be equal to *two* Unbelievers. Here we are, so to speak, taken into the Prophet's study ; the Surah is re-edited with a necessary modification.

At times where such references are given, they only produce fresh enigmas. So in a matter with which we shall presently deal, we find Surah xvi. 119 quote a list of foods forbidden to the Jews which is to be found in Surah vi. 147 ; whereas Surah vi. 146 equally clearly quotes a list of foods forbidden to Moslems which is given in Surah xvi. 116. The explanation of such a case can only be found in the repetition of the same matter differently arranged, which we have seen to be characteristic of the lecture as opposed to the book.

The stories furnished by later writers of the mode wherein the Ḳoran was edited are all clearly affected by the practice of the traditionalists, and little credit attaches to them. All that we can gather of the editor's method is that he intended to be as objective as possible ; *i.c.* to leave the employment of the sacred volume as free as possible to the Moslem community. For since the doctrine that parts of the work abrogated other parts was openly acknowledged, any suspicion of chronological arrangement would settle the important question, which texts were abrogated.   And possibly this accounts for the mixture in the same Surahs of matter belonging to different years: as in Surah iii. there are verses which must have been delivered in the third year of the Hijrah, commenting on the battle of Uḥud, to which are prefixed a series of verses clearly dealing with Christian controversy, and doubtless rightly assigned to a much later period.   The text which claims to be the last in the Koran, " This day I have completed your religion," is not put at the end but in the middle of the volume.   The verse which has every appearance of being the first text revealed is stowed away not far from the end, and evidently, short as is the Surah wherein it is inserted, mixed with matter belonging to a different period.   We cannot say either why in certain cases several texts are put together to form a chapter, whereas towards the end of the volume we have a series of Surahs limited to a very few verses apiece.

Since the collector of the Koran left no memoirs and composed no preface, we do not otherwise know precisely how he worked, or on what principle he admitted, arranged, and generally dealt with his matter.   We know that some portions of the Koran must have been taught for ritual purposes, but cannot say exactly which.   From a story to the effect that ‘Ā’ishah, when quoting the Koran at her trial, had forgotten the name of Joseph's father, we should gather that the Surah of Joseph, perhaps the most continuous of the whole series, was familiarly known at the time, yet not so familiarly but that a member of the Prophet's household might be only moderately well acquainted with its contents. But though we are unable to pronounce on the skill displayed by the editor of the Koran, there is a strong probability that most of the matter which he collected had been actually delivered by the Prophet. The case which has been quoted, where the utterance of-one Surah is confirmed by another, and apologised for in a third and a fourth, gives the very strongest presumption of genuineness. Moreover, the controversies wherewith it largely, or rather mainly, deals were stale at the time when the collection was made. Much of it deals with Jewish controversy; the Judaism of Arabia had been effectively silenced by the Prophet before the taking of Meccah. The prophecy in Surah iii. that the Jews would be humiliated was fulfilled before the Prophet's time in Medinah had half expired; the flourishing Jewish communities had been exterminated or impoverished. Both the admiration and the denunciation of the Banu Israil, with which so many of the Surahs deal, had sunk from the region of practice to that of reminiscence or of theory, ever since the battle of the Trench. Scarcely less out of date was the polemic against idolatry; for by the Prophet's death the idols had been destroyed, and though we hear of false prophets arising in Arabia, and of rebellion against the Medinese yoke, there appears to have been no recrudescence of paganism.

Only in one case do we find that the collector of

the Koran embodied what looks like a state paper, viz. the manifesto to the Arabs which forms at any rate the commencement of Surah ix., which, for some reason, lacks the invocation that is prefixed to all the other Surahs. It calls itself " Licence issued by Allah and His Apostle to the Pagans with whom you have made a covenant," and is evidently a copy of an actual document sent to Meccah. The co-ordination of Allah and the Apostle as authors of the document is unique, and makes it appear that in the period when it was issued the Koran had come to be considered as the Prophet's official utterances; and that the theory of double personality, according to which the Prophet at times represented the Deity and at other times himself, yet was to be obeyed in the latter capacity no less than in the former, was making its appearance. So far as this manifesto is in the name of the Prophet it should perhaps have found no place in the Koran. Elsewhere it is hard to say to what extent manuscript materials were employed.

Our belief, then, in the general genuineness of the Koran rests on the agreement of its contents with what would be expected if the account of its genesis and collection were true. The greater part of the collection is likely to have been delivered orally, and indeed the matter is declared to have been sent down to the Prophet's heart to deliver with his tongue. The material was, as perhaps is the case with most preachers, meagre; he was acquainted with only a few stories, and the doctrines which he had to communicate were during a long period exceedingly simple. Whether improvised or prepared, and probably both methods were employed, these discourses impressed many hearers, and were recollected in different forms. In accounts of dialogues and public discourses, both real and fictitious, we find authors who lived before the invention of printing speak of the report as put together from the accounts of hearers, and we not unfrequently meet the assumption that a hearer of an oration will remember it, and be able to repeat it. Such reports of the Prophet's sermons must have been found in the minds or hands of various Believers, and in the later Medinese period a reading public may have begun to exist.

The Koran, then, was what remained to take the place of the Prophet, and the dead letter is a poor substitute in any case for the living voice. In the Prophet's time the divine ordinances could be changed from day to day; after his death they became stereotyped for ever. " Do you doubt," asks a catechist rather more than a hundred years after that event, " that the Koran was brought down to the Prophet by Gabriel the faithful spirit: that therein God had declared what is lawful and unlawful, prescribed His rules and established His practices, and told the history of the past and of the future to the end of time ? "[1] The catechumen replies, " I doubt not." This particular sect held, indeed, that there was somewhere an esoteric tradition whereby it could be supplemented, some person or persons who might deal with it some-

[1] Ṭabarī ii. 1961.

what as the Prophet had dealt with its divine original ; but the greater part of Islam rejected this doctrine, and so closed the avenue, little used, it must be admitted, to possible improvements.   Yet in some way the community had to be supplied with something more than was contained in the fragments put together by the first Caliph's order: with law, ritual, morals, theology, and even history.   The task before us is to trace these several supplements to their source.

LECTURE II

SOME twelve years are said to have elapsed between
the collecting of the Koran, which is supposed to have
been executed by order and for the use of the first
successor of the Prophet, and the issuing of an official
edition.   In the meantime it would appear that unofficial texts must have been promulgated, of which,
however, little more than the rumour reaches us ;
different families were supposed to possess their own
recensions, and this was likely to lead to serious mischief.   The third successor of the Prophet had all
these texts collected and either burned or washed out
—a more economical process, permitting the use of
the material for some other purpose ; in their place
authorised copies were sent to the chief Islamic cities.
It is asserted that even the fair copy which had been
made by the second successor, and after his death had
got into the possession of his daughter, was obtained
from her heir and destroyed.   So valuable a relic
would not have been so treated had not its preservation been dangerous to someone.   Little is said by
the Islamic historians of this act, which, however, must
have been in the highest degree sensational ; for the

Koran-readers were developing into a profession, and doubtless possessed in their Korans a lucrative asset. Yet since the destruction of the earlier copies was effectively carried out, the Moslems are compelled to assume that the text which remains is authoritative; for otherwise they would be casting doubts on the basis of their system. The act of Othman is therefore commended by the historians who mention it, and the use of non-Othmanic readings was afterwards punishable with death; [1] though whether his contemporaries regarded it in the same light may well be doubted. Among the charges brought against Othman by those who afterwards besieged him in Medinah and murdered him, one is that he found the Korans many and left one; [2] and that he had "torn up the Book"; [3] and for a long time his enemies called him "the tearer of the Books." [4] The party who are associated with his assassination are sometimes called "the Readers." [5] The reason alleged for this drastic measure is the fear that different readings would lead to the development of sectarianism, this having happened in the Christian Church; although it might not be easy to demonstrate that the various readings of the Bible had effected much in this direction; and Othman's expedient by no means proved itself effective, since sects developed in Islam with great rapidity. The story of the destruction of

[1] Yākūt, *Dictionary of Learned Men*, vi. 300, 499.

[2] Tabarī i. 2952, 10.   [3] *Ibid.*, ii. 516, 5.

[4] *Ibid.*, ii. 747, anno 67.

[5] i. 3323, 15. The charge that he was the first who altered the Prophet's *sunnah* seems an echo of this. Aghani xx. 101, 14.

Omar's copy suggests that the official edition contained matter which current copies did not contain; and, indeed, we may easily believe that the text did not escape interpolation during the period which separated the ultimate edition from the original collection.[1] The first successor is said to have composed a text wherein the Prophet's death is foretold, and a little tampering with the sacred volume is likely to have been executed from time to time. Some verses which give the appearance of being post-Mohammedan are a set which recognise a distinction between two classes of texts in the Koran: those which have been revised and those which are equivocal. This division seems unnecessary when the doctrine of abrogation has been adopted; nor while the Prophet lived can we well believe that any portion of the Koran was equivocal, for he was there to interpret it. Further, the word "clear" or "perspicuous," used as the contrary of "equivocal," is so frequently employed of the Koran that he would probably have disapproved the use of the latter term except in the sense of "uniform," in which signification it is indeed applied to the Koran as a whole.

Besides this, the Koran is treated as a unit, which it can never have been while the Prophet lived: the well of revelation had not then run dry. Further, the revised texts are here said to be the " Mother of the Book "; but that phrase as used by the Prophet means

---

[1] One sect of Khawārij declared Surah xii. (Joseph) spurious. Ghunyah i. 76. The Ibāḍites charge Othman with having "altered God's word." Sachau, *Anschauungen der Ibaditen*, p. 53.

something very different, viz. the divine original, the copy in the possession of the Celestial Author, who is at liberty to revise as He will. Hence this passage seems intended to deal with difficulties which can scarcely have cropped up while the Prophet lived, but necessarily arose when the letter had to take the place of the living intermediary between God and man.

A controversy on which we never seem to hear the last word is whether or not the Alexandrian library was burned by the Moslem conquerors; and even as late as 1912 some severe language has been heard about it. The real difficulty about the story is—What is meant by the Alexandrian library? but the important question from some points of view is whether the belief that the Koran rendered all other literature dangerous or superfluous was or was not current at the time when this disaster is supposed to have taken place. Now, that the Moslems wilfully destroyed books belonging to other communities, composed in foreign languages, is not credible; they would not have regarded the preservation of such literature as a matter affecting themselves. But the rise of the Islamic state was an occasion which would naturally have produced a mass of literature, each person recording what he knew of the remarkable man who had founded the Arabian empire, or of the campaigns which had brought such brilliant results; yet those who in later times endeavoured to discover what was the first book written after the Koran give us a selection of authors whose death-dates come between the years 149–160 of the Migration; and

though a work by an author who died in 110 is sometimes mentioned, it would seem that its genuineness
is ordinarily denied. Of those prose works which have
come down to us, little is earlier than 150, and
literature begins to accumulate in masses only after
another decade or two. Thus the first actual treatises
on jurisprudence as a science were those of Shāfiʻī,
who flourished in the second half of the second
century ; previously the science had been locked up
with its possessors.[1]

Considerable vagueness, in consequence, attaches
to the history of the first century and a half, and even
in the case of events of primary importance we are
confronted with puzzles. We cannot, however, credit
the whole Moslem population with inability to express
themselves otherwise than in lyric verse. The long
silence of the Arabs under Islam is to be accounted
for by the importance attached to the Koran, which,
it was thought, no more tolerated other books beside
itself than Allah tolerated other deities. The claim
which, according to the story of the Alexandrian
library, was made by Omar for the Koran does not
exceed what it claims for itself. It is " a detailed
account of everything."[2] It was delivered in a night
wherein every difficult matter was distinguished.[3]
" We have neglected nothing in the Book."[4] Now,
a " detailed account of everything," " a Book wherein
nothing is neglected," clearly renders all other litera-

---

[1] Yākūt vi. 388.   In the Iḥyā al-ʻUlūm i. 65 this matter is discussed ; see also Ithāf i. 434.
[2] Surah xii. 111.   [3] xliv. 3.   [4] vi. 38.

ture superfluous or dangerous; and, indeed, when Bonaparte asked some sheikhs whether the Koran in its complete account of everything included formulæ for the casting of cannon and making of gunpowder, they had to reply that it did, though they admitted that not every reader would 'know how to find them. Hence, it would seem, Moslems were precluded from composing books, and references to others than the Koran in the early generations of Islam are rare. Such references are usually to such as contained oracles; thus a son of the conqueror of Egypt, when in that country, read the works of Daniel, and made prophetic calculations on its data;[1] but even these books appear to be ordinarily in the hands of Jews and Christians,[2] or in those of converted Israelites, who may have retained them from their earlier days.[3] Even letters were ordinarily brief or rather laconic; the first author of prolix epistles comes into history in the year 60, only, however, to have his despatch rejected for one which was conciser.[4] Attempts at preserving history seem to have taken the form of tribal narratives, to which reference is sometimes made;[5] these were recited in the home,[6] or more often in the mosques, and at times some particular mosque was a favourite resort of such narrators.[7]

These narrators are not easily distinguished from preachers, who (sometimes after the afternoon prayer[8])

---

[1] Ṭabarī ii. 399, anno 61.
[2] *Ibid.*, ii. 1138, 1464.
[3] *Ibid.*, ii. 786, anno 68.
[4] *Ibid.*, ii. 270 ('Amr b. Nāfiʿ).
[5] *Ibid.*, ii. 856, 1180.
[6] *Ibid.*, ii. 1919.
[7] *Ibid.*, ii. 455, 656.
[8] *Ibid.*, ii. 1968.

were employed by commanders to inspirit the troops by recounting to them the wars of the Lord and the merits of the Holy Family.[1] Probably it was in the recitations of these "narrators," as they were called, that the bulk of the Prophet's biography was preserved, whence the ordinary Moslem obtained a general acquaintance with it and would understand allusions to its details.[2] The profession of "narrator" does not appear to have been originally distinct from that of Koran-reader and jurist.[3] A jurist was the author of one of the earliest attempts at written history of which we hear, viz. a list of the Caliphs with their ages; though its author died as early as 124 A.H., many of his figures were uncertain;[4] and contradictory accounts have been handed down to us with respect to the dates of highly important events. In general, if anything was taken down, the copy would appear to have been retained only until its contents had been committed to memory; and the author of this chronological table is said to have been exceptional in taking down matter that was not strictly juristic.[5] He became, indeed, thereby the greatest scholar of his time; but it was not in his power to compensate for the want of contemporary histories, or to discriminate between the basis of fact and the accumulations brought about by the process of narration.

The notion that the sacred book is the whole of

---

[1] Ṭabarī ii. 949, 950, 1055.   [2] *Ibid.,* ii. 231, 1226, 1242, 1338.
[3] *Ibid.,* ii. 1086.   [4] *Ibid.,* ii. 428.
[5] Jāḥiẓ, Bayān ii. 26.

the national literature has been too often current for us to be surprised at the Moslems adopting it. A Koranic theory is that every nation has its book—naturally one only.[1] With whatever sanctity a text may be surrounded, probably the only way to effectually guard it against rivals is to prevent the possibility of rivalry. The Jews interpreted a verse near the end of Ecclesiastes as definitely forbidding the addition of anything to their national literature; and for three parts of a millennium they observed this precept faithfully. Hence the national history of that race between the fall of Jerusalem and the foundation of Baghdad is a blank. The Apocalypse ends with a terrible threat against those who venture to make any addition to the prophecy of this book, which may indeed refer to that particular collection of oracles, but is quite likely to be interpreted of putting anything at all that is to be permanent on writing material. Possibly there were fewer scruples among Moslems about the writing of poetry, to which there are occasional allusions,[2] since such compositions were by their form clearly distinguished from the Koran. We have seen that some scruples were felt about collecting the Koran itself; it need not then surprise us that there were yet greater scruples about collecting anything else. And if, as was the case, even those Scriptures which the Koran professed to confirm and corroborate might not be put into the hands of Moslems, still less, we can imagine, might any other form of literature; though it seems clear

[1] Surah xlv. 27.   [2] Ṭabarī ii. 1732.

that the Prophet had no idea that any other form of literature existed. But even had he known of it, it is improbable that his attitude would have been altered thereby; for his system, as might be expected of a man who was by instinct a military commander, was decidedly one of short cuts. This appears clearly in his calendar. The brains of mathematicians and astronomers had been wearied with endeavours to find a formula which would harmonise the supposed motions of the sun and the moon; Mohammed settles the whole difficulty in a moment by declaring that the year in God's estimation is one of twelve lunar months. Christianity had been rent to pieces with the difficulty of formulating the nature of Christ, whose mother, it was agreed, was a virgin; Mohammed settles the matter straight off: the nature of Christ is like that of Adam. Now, when difficulties can be settled with this directness, clearly research is useless; for the students of these matters had arrived at nothing so simple. And the Koran makes statements on so many subjects that its claim to settle everything is at least plausible. We can learn from it where the sun sinks, and where it rises; that the period from birth to weaning is two years, and from conception to weaning thirty months; besides a précis of Old Testament and New Testament history, it is generally encyclopædic in its range of information.

But whether the collection of Surahs was intended as a manual of either ritual or law, civil and criminal, or of ethics, its utility was decidedly limited. In the first place, there is no principle of arrangement, whence the whole book must be perused in order to find the enactment on any subject.   In the second place, the enactments on the same subject are apt to be numerous and contradictory.   We may take the case of lawful foods.   In Surah xxii. certain beasts are declared lawful, " except what shall be read unto you "—where there is thus a promise of further information.   In Surah xvi. 116 such information is given : here the exceptions are four—" God has made unlawful for you that which has died a natural death, blood, swine's flesh, and what has been consecrated to any other than Allah."   It must be confessed that the classification leaves something to be desired ; and, indeed, some argued that the fat of swine was lawful according to the wording of this text.   In vi. 119 we are told that the details have been given, only it is there explained that " what has been consecrated to any other than Allah " means " what has not had Allah's name mentioned over it."   And in verse 146 the Prophet is told to say that in what has been revealed to him he finds nothing forbidden save the four things mentioned in Surah xvi.   In Surah ii. 168 the same list is given again.   In Surah v., however, the first verse tells us that graminivorous beasts are lawful food, except what shall be read unto you, and the list follows in verse 4 : but here no fewer than six fresh exceptions are added.   Since there follows the expression, " To-day I have completed for you your religion," it may be reasonably inferred that this is the final utterance on the subject of lawful and un-lawful food ; but one feels that the assertion in

Surah vi., " I only find in what has been revealed to me," followed by the shorter list, ought not to have been left unmodified by an editor; for though the statement in Surah v. may well be the final utterance on the subject, it contradicts Surah vi. Since, then, the verse in Surah vi. is abrogated, it ought either to have been omitted, or some chronological note should have been appended; and, indeed, in Surah vi., which takes its name from these beasts, the author goes out of his way to give what he supposes to be the Jewish law as well as that of his own community, and to this revelation reference is made in Surah xvi.

Now, if on a matter which admits of such precision as this, the ruling of the Koran is inconsistent and self-contradictory, we cannot reasonably expect precision on those moral and metaphysical questions which taxed the ability even of an Aristotle, who to his natural endowments had added a long and profound study of the theory of classification.

To speak of the metaphysics of the Koran might seem to be an anachronism, but the evidence which justifies our using the phrase is irrefragable. It repeatedly attributes the unbelief of its opponents to the act of God; a man's acceptance of Islam is said to be due to God's expanding his breast (vi. 125), his refusal of it to his breast being straitened: God has rendered such a person deaf and blind, and sealed up his brains so that he cannot make use of them. Had God willed, everyone on earth without exception would have believed (x. 99); no soul can believe save by the permission of God (100); he, Mohammed, cannot force people to believe; his preaching would be unavailing if God willed to lead people astray (xi. 36). It was impossible to rescue those who were doomed to punishment (xxxix. 20). To all this there was the obvious retort on the part of the Unbelievers that they too could not alter what God had decreed (vi. 149, xvi. 37); "had God willed, neither we nor our forefathers would have been pagans, nor should we have declared any lawful food unlawful." And this objection is repeatedly recorded. The only reply that the Koran can offer is that Unbelievers in old times said the same, and that the people who say this have no real knowledge, but are only guessing.

With regard to morals there is the same difficulty. The Koran certainly is consistent on one point, the first commandment, " Thou shalt have none other gods but Me "; and this is practically the sole message which all the prophets communicate. If we come to other commandments, we have to read through the whole work in order to be sure what is actually meant. Where something analogous to a code is given, *e.g.* in Surah vi. 152 and following, Surah xvii. 24, xxv. 65 following, Surah xxxi. 12, Surah xvi. 92, the second commandment is usually " kindness to parents "; but then comes the difficulty noticed in the case of Abraham: what happens if the parent is an Unbeliever? In Surah xxix. 7 the injunction is followed by the rider, " But if they urge thee to associate with Me that concerning which thou hast no knowledge, then obey them not"; in xxxi. 14 there is added to this, "But associate with them kindly." But in Surah lx., when, owing to the Migration and the battle of Badr, this matter has assumed serious proportions, the Moslems are told to declare that there is perpetual enmity between them and the Unbelievers, whatever the relationship; Abraham's promise to pray for his father is stated to be an exception which is not to be imitated.

We see, then, that the second commandment has had to undergo serious alteration as time goes on; and without the theory of abrogation it is impossible to make use of Koranic rulings on the commandment concerning the honour due to parents. With other commandments we can trace the same process. In the code of Surah xvi. 93 there is a commandment to keep oaths; but in Surah v. 91 this rule is modified by the introduction of the principle of compensation, whereby the violation of an oath may be atoned by some other performance; and in Surah lxvi. this new principle is confirmed and applied to a case wherein the Prophet himself is concerned. The tendency here, then, as in the former case, is towards laxity; and it has had the decidedly serious result that there appears to be no mode known to Mohammedan law whereby an oath can be made legally binding; for not only does the Koran expressly state that the performance of certain charitable acts will serve as a substitute for specific performance, but the Prophet is credited with the maxim according to which if a man having taken an oath to do something discovers some preferable course, he is to take that preferable course and make compensation.   And, indeed, the jurists appear to devote their attention entirely to the nature of the compensation to be adopted in such cases, without disputing the legality of perjury.   It cannot, however, be easily believed that the Prophet would have failed to see the danger of admitting this principle unrestrictedly, though there may be cases in which the existence of an authority empowered to release men from such obligations is conceivably desirable.

If in lieu of a code we endeavour to collect occasional precepts or to analyse the general spirit of the Koran, the result is somewhat wanting in precision and consistency.   It is clearly an untenable view that the moral law can vary with the varying conditions of an individual or of a community; it may be wise to fight with Unbelievers only when there is a good chance of defeating them, but the question whether it is right or not to do so cannot be settled on this ground.   On this subject, however, we have a series of utterances which steadily increase in intolerance until they culminate in the ferocious document that forms Surah ix.   We can indeed gauge the agitation of the Prophet in that Surah by the fact that he mentions a battle-field by name— Hunain; elsewhere he uses veiled phrases, *e.g.* the day of Deliverance, or the day when the two parties met.   Similarly, in the disagreeable episode connected with his adopted son, he goes so far as to mention Zaid by name.   Still, it is not possible to harmonise a precept which forbids any sort of dispute, a precept which urges the rendering of good for evil, and a precept which enjoins the extermination of pagans, fighting with them wherever they are to be found, disregarding all family ties when religion is concerned. If we admit the theory that God's commands are dictates of prudence, *i.e.* are temporary rules accommodated to the varying circumstances of a few days or years, the question suggests itself: did circumstances cease to change on the Prophet's death? Changing so quickly within the twenty years of his activity that the rule which suited the first year was wholly inapplicable in the last, can they in the last year have become so stereotyped that no further alteration is required?

Just, then, as we find that metaphysical difficulties are not really abstruse, but on the surface as well as in the depth, so the problems suggested by the theory of revelation formulated themselves even to untrained minds. The Prophet's answer is that of a dictator, who sees no difficulty about altering his rulings from day to day; the texts which had ceased to be applicable were wiped out, erased, and something equally good if not better substituted for them.

Even with regard to ritual we are confronted by the same difficulties. Doubtless the Koran consistently enjoins prayer and alms, and it certainly prescribes the pilgrimage to the Ancient House; yet it is agreed that the Koran cannot be quoted for the number and exact nature of the ceremonies which together constitute prayer, or even for a complete definition of what is meant by ceremonial washing. Of the system which occupies so many pages in the law-books, and of the minute details connected with this performance, only the beginnings can be found in the Koran; and it is by no means certain that the prescriptions in that book which are concerned with nightly prayer are meant to apply to anyone but the Prophet himself. Similarly, though charity is constantly enjoined, and the alms spoken of as an institution, there is no guidance as to the amount to be paid. Slightly more detail perhaps is given of the ceremonies connected with the pilgrimage which it was the intention of the Prophet to preserve or to abolish; but even on this subject the statements are scanty. It is probably true that in the Prophet's time none of these "pillars of Islam," as they are termed, assumed quite as stereotyped a shape as that into which the studies of the first century of the Migration brought them; yet where the leading principle of a system is that one particular teacher should be obeyed and imitated, the accurate formulation of duties is evidently required. If prayer and alms are performances which God demands, it becomes necessary to know what constitutes them; where there is a claim to be satisfied, the debtor should know the exact amount of the claim. Since God is, according to the Koran, "quick at accounts," the debtor must also have an opportunity of keeping his own. Moreover, the alms being a tax which the sovereign has to collect, its amount must be definitely known.

In the third place, it is clear that the legislation of the Koran is imperfect, and fails to deal with numerous subjects on which rules are required. Such a subject is constitutional law, the principle whereon the ruler or sovereign is appointed, and the limits of his power. When a dispute concerning the succession arose, the only Koranic text which seemed to deal with the matter was one referring to disputes arising between a man and his wife, in which case an umpire was to be appointed from either side; what was to happen in the event of these umpires disagreeing was not specified. Those who were appointed to decide the succession to the throne were enjoined to settle the matter according to the Koran, if this were possible; to do so was found quite impracticable, though it would appear that one of the parties endeavoured to effect this by extending the principle of analogy which had already been employed in the case of the arbitrators. It was then argued that where a murder had been committed, " authority " was given to the avenger of blood, *i.e.* the kinsman on whom that duty naturally fell; and the word " authority " might conceivably apply to general authority, though the context would be against this. The occurrence, however, of this text, which might thus have some bearing on the question of the successor to the murdered Othman, was probably what encouraged one of the parties to stake its cause on the ruling of the Koran.

If the Prophet's mission was analogous to what he supposed that of Jesus to have been, *i.e.* the relaxation of some parts of an earlier code, but in general the maintenance of it, it would have been natural for the community to adopt the codes in use among either Jews or Christians, merely introducing such changes as the new revelation had brought.   And, indeed, the academic question is sometimes posed: are we bound by the codes of our predecessors?   The question is clearly academic, for there is practically no mode of getting at those codes.   The doctrine that the Jewish and Christian scriptures had been wilfully corrupted beyond recognition seems to have become a dogma of Islam at a very early date: it is the regular apology for the astounding diversity of the Koran in matters of history from the Christian and Jewish documents, and any system which involved the employment of those scriptures had necessarily to be rejected.   It will be seen that this theory is actually made a principle of law, and regulates the relations of the Moslem government with its Christian subjects.

Still, though the nature of the Koran was not such as to render it a convenient handbook for consultation on the various difficulties which arose, there were certain sources of information which for a time might be utilised.   The Prophet had governed a community a sufficient length of time in a variety of circumstances for the Moslem life to have developed in a particular way, and for Islam itself to have exhibited what might be called a spirit; the Prophet's career had for some years at least been in miniature what was to be the career of his successors: the conquest and administration of provinces. And, on the other hand, from the different conditions wherein he had lived with his followers, there was more than a general notion current of what he approved and disapproved. Victorious over internal and external enemies, recognised as absolute dictator on all questions connected with morality and law, he had been free to do as he liked; there was little reason to suppose that greater success would have seriously changed his methods. Hence there was already a style or system which admitted of continuation.

One result was, then, to make the Moslems hero-worshippers to a greater degree than any other community has attained. The Koran bids its devotees take as their models those who have been guided, and in particular urges that the Prophet is a pattern of conduct. Naturally, his immediate associates were supposed to have resembled him most closely, and what they did became a norm of conduct far below, indeed, that which was attributed to the Prophet, but at least analogous to it; whoso followed their example could not go wrong. This principle eventually developed into a cult of saints, with numerous extraordinary superstitions. Moslem essays have a tendency to consist of citations of sayings bearing on the subject which are attributed to the Companions of the Prophet. But though much of this matter, if not the whole of it, is apocryphal, we cannot doubt that the mode of life pursued by the Prophet exercised a great influence on his environment, and the process spread through the ever-expanding area of Islam.   During the early generations the character thus disseminated was fairly preserved ; as time went on and the state became more settled, it became remodelled, and its old features were blurred ; but some were too clearly cut to be rendered indistinguishable.   And in the encomia which certain historians bestow on Moslem sovereigns, and their assessment of the conduct which they record, they retain the old valuations derived from a study of the lives of the Prophet and the foremost of the Companions.

If, leaving theory, we turn to practice, and endeavour to picture to ourselves the life of the earliest Moslems, the Companions of the Prophet, who occupy in this system the same place as is occupied in Christianity by Apostles and Saints, we shall probably understand the ethical value of the Koran better than if we study it with orthodox commentaries.   These persons accepted the Koran as guidance at the time of its author or at any rate authorised expounder.   What effect had it on their lives ?   Two qualities it certainly encouraged : courage and discipline.   The Prophet spared neither himself nor his followers ; they fought many a battle at great odds and won.   The boast of the Koran that a Believer was worth two Unbelievers on the battle-field, if not ten, justified itself repeatedly.   Not only the Jews, whose religion disarms them, but the legions of the Greek and Persian empires, were unable to face the Believers' onslaught.

The heroic life, as depicted in the Greek Iliad, bears

a close resemblance to the life of the early Moslems; they fight in tribes, and the capable fighter is the tribal hero. Nor is the religious basis entirely dissimilar; the loves and hates of the fighters in both cases are the loves and hates of their gods. The best fighter is also the best worshipper. But it follows from this proposition that the best worshipper is often the best fighter; and the government is to a certain extent priestly in consequence. When the Yemenite tribes at Kufah were making common cause against the usurper Mukhtār, the rivalry between their chieftains was likely to lead to disaster; the affair was settled by making the chief of the Readers, *i.e.* the person best acquainted with the Koran, leader of prayer and so leader of the forces.[1]

The experiences of the Prophet's life, the constant bloodshed which marked his career at Medinah, seem to have impressed his followers with a profound belief in the value of bloodshed as opening the gates of Paradise. Among the many pathetic stories which Tabarī has preserved is that of the Penitents, inhabitants of Kufah who had invited the Prophet's grandson Husain to come and be their sovereign, but, owing to the vigorous measures of the Umayyad governor of Kufah, left Husain in the lurch, who was presently surrounded by the Umayyad troops at Kerbela, where he and many members of his family met their deaths. The death of Husain has been to a large portion of the Moslem world the analogue of the Crucifixion: the culminating crime of the whole

---

[1] Tabarī ii. 654.

world, too horrible to mention, yet always to be kept in mind. When these Penitents became conscious of the offence which they had committed, they decided that they durst not appear before their Creator without having taken steps to atone for it; they must take the life of those by whose hands Ḥusain had fallen. When they had taken this resolution, there was already a considerable reaction against the Umayyads, for indeed the slaughter of the Prophet's household was eminently calculated to produce one; the authorities in Kufah promised the Penitents their aid and support, merely desiring that this endeavour to avenge Ḥusain should be undertaken with caution and prudence; only the Penitents declined. It appeared that their desire was far more to lose their own lives in the pursuit of their aim than to compass that aim; an avenue to Paradise was opened to them, and they hastened to take it. On their way to battle with the Umayyad forces they met other sympathisers, who also urged caution, and deprecated unnecessary waste of life, and especially of noble lives; the sympathisers were thanked, but their assistance and their counsel declined. On the battle-field many were offered amnesty by their fellow-tribesmen who happened to be in the Umayyad army; in the cases quoted the amnesty was declined; the Penitents fought till they fell. Similarly, we read of generals who, hurrying to battle, asked their friends to pray for their martyrdom;[1] and of those who, mortally wounded

---

[1] Ṭabarī ii. 644, 16.

in battle, expired congratulating themselves that they were dying in the mode they best desired.[1] The Caliph Ibn Zubair finds consolation for the death of his brother on the battle-field in the fact that he is following the family tradition; unlike the Umayyads, who regularly died in their beds.[2] Other men as they reach old age anxiously seize what may be their last chance of martyrdom.[3] This spirit seems to have regularly animated the Khawārij, the most ferocious as well as the most pious of the Moslems.[4] They were habitually able to defeat many times their number in consequence. But it also animated those who extended the Islamic empire to the far East.[5]

But beyond these virtues, courage and discipline, it might be difficult to find any which the Companions of the Prophet exhibited above other men. Temperance, in the sense of total abstinence, was part of their discipline; the amount of chastity demanded was very slight. The ordinary ills of humanity, envy, hatred, and malice, seem to have been rife even in the Prophet's household, and the Shi'ites seem historically correct in asserting that after his death his staff subordinated all other considerations to an intrigue for the succession. Where the goods of infidels were in view, the precept " Thou shalt not covet " does not appear to have been enjoined; and the thirst at any rate for infidel blood was encouraged rather than suppressed. Those who had to deal with the Prophet or his immediate suc-

---

[1] Ṭabarī ii. 657. [2] ii. 819. [3] ii. 1037.
[4] ii. 1378. [5] ii. 1604.

cessors in Medinah had to deal with an armed camp:
with a fighting force as effective as has ever been
organised, when fighting depended not on brain
power but on physical force. The Prophet rightly
claims to have set a good example in resolution and
contempt of danger and fatigue. But that any of
the gentler virtues were cultivated does not appear;
and the vices which are associated with Asiatic
despotisms seem to have displayed themselves from
the time when the despotism of Medinah was
founded. The Prophet's successor and bosom friend,
according to the best authorities, deprived the
Prophet's daughter of her property in order to
avenge an insult which his own daughter had received
some years before. And, in general, little love seems
to have been lost between the Companions of the
Prophet.

The shedding of blood, indeed, became a passion
which at times assumed strange shapes. The sect of
Khawārij or professional rebels, which was called after
al-Azraḳ, made a point of killing women and children
as well as male Moslems who would not accept their
symbol; a letter is extant wherein this practice is
justified from the Koran: these monsters spared
Christians and Jews.[1] In the civil wars at times
some of the conquerors could see that the Moslems
whom they had defeated were brave men, who could
ill be spared for the defence of the frontiers, and that
it was improper to treat the prisoners of war as
responsible for the deaths of the victor's comrades;

----

[1] See, *e.g.*, Ṭabarī ii. 760.

but such voices were rarely able to convince: the thirst for blood was too strong. When the adventurer Mukhtār undertook to avenge the death of Ḥusain, he slaughtered hundreds, meaning to kill all the troops that had been engaged against Ḥusain; the real head of the house of Ali advised him to spill less blood. A pious insurgent in the year 76 advised his leader to kill all who disagreed with him before even summoning them to a change.[1] And some of his followers carried out this principle without even consulting their commanders.[2] The less religious, *e.g.* the founder of the Umayyad dynasty, seem to have developed this horrible taste less than the devotees; but even their record is terrible. We cannot fail to find the source of this most painful feature of Islam throughout its history in the Prophet's massacres of his opponents, and in the theory of the Koran that copious bloodshed is characteristic of a true prophet at a certain stage of his career.

Dangerous consequences were drawn from the Prophet's doctrine, emphasised on the occasion of a domestic irregularity, that an oath might be cancelled by some substituted performance. According to the tradition, one of the Companions of the Prophet, Zubair, who had started the revolt against Ali, was persuaded by the latter to abandon his project, and gave what seemed a solemn oath, that he would not take part in a war against the Caliph. Zubair's son, who afterwards endeavoured to maintain himself as

<hr>

[1] Ṭabarī ii. 886.   [2] *Ibid.*, ii. 975.

sovereign, persuaded his father to make atonement for his oath by freeing a slave, and take his place in the battle-field as if nothing had happened. The unscrupulous adventurer Mukhtār, who by posing as the avenger of Ḥusain shed blood in rivers, had been imprisoned by the governor of Kufah, when some suspicion of his plans leaked out; owing to the intercession of Omar's highly respected son, the governor was persuaded to give Mukhtār his liberty, but not before making him take the most solemn oaths that he would not head an insurrection. Mukhtār, we are told, readily took the oaths offered, thinking to himself what a fool the governor of Kufah must be to suppose an oath could make any difference, when it was so easy to substitute some other performance for it; particularly as it might easily be maintained that taking vengeance for the death of Ḥusain was a duty which took precedence of all others. Like Zubair, then, Mukhtār perjured himself without scruple. Yet in perjuring themselves they had the authority of the Koran behind them, and were acting well within the law. The oath of a Moslem sovereign or commander was worth nothing at all, though public opinion seems sometimes to have been moved by very flagrant violations.

Still, it is possible to formulate some more general theory of the spirit which animated the Prophet himself, and with which he endeavoured to impress his followers. The political philosophers of the East inform us that men follow the religion of their sovereigns, and imitation of the Prophet, which the later Moslems carry on according to their lights, is repeatedly enjoined in the Koran. Certain rights doubtless belonged to his office, and there are revelations which deal with this matter; the Believers are not' to treat him as one of themselves, and are to observe in their dealings with him something of the etiquette usual in courts. But, discovering what his spirit is, they are to animate themselves so far as possible with the same.

The spirit of Islam as it appears in the Koran might be said to be *Moderation.* Although the Prophet may have had falsely attributed to him the saying, " The best of things are the mean," he would probably have accepted the doctrine with little hesitation. With regard to devotional acts he is credited with the saying, " The best religious observance is the least cumbersome," and he is supposed to have forbidden various extravagances in this matter. Where charity towards relations and beggars is enjoined, the Koran adds, " Yet do be not lavish; the spendthrifts are brethren of Satan, who was ungrateful to his lord. Do not tie your hand to your neck, and do not open it to its full width " (xvii. 28–31). In the list of the virtuous (xxv. 67) are those who when they spend are not lavish and not stingy, but on the right line between the two. In managing the goods of orphans the poor trustee is told he may take a little for himself, but is not to be wasteful (iv. 6). If a tribesman has been murdered, retaliation is permissible, but the avenger of blood should not perpetrate a massacre (xvii. 35). Feasting

is recommended on certain days, but there should
be no excess (vii. 29).   Chastity is repeatedly recommended, but there is no objection to unlimited
concubinage.   The " people of the book " are blamed
for fanaticism in their religion (v. 81).

In the time of the Prophet himself these somewhat
homely precepts were modified by the enthusiasm of
fighting and conquest.   Although it appears that he
fainted the first time that he saw blood shed, he very
soon got over that weakness, and probably was never
so happy as on the battle-field.   The portions of the
Koran which deal with the sacred war exhibit the
spirit which fills the song of Deborah, with its scorn
for all weakness and irresolution, its contempt of all
excuses for staying away from the conflict, and its
admiration for those who fight to the death, who
neither ask nor give quarter.   And for the rising
state this quality was so desirable that the Prophet
appears to have pardoned many a peccadillo in those
who displayed it to the full.   Like other Arab
chieftains he was perpetually engaged in warfare ;
only by organisation and discipline he ensured
success, by fighting with a steady imperialistic aim
he grew stronger instead of weaker after each engage-
ment, and his promise of Paradise to those who fell
evoked a kind of enthusiasm which went beyond
anything which paganism had been able to arouse.

Down to the end of the Prophet's life the dogma
of Islam was still rather negative than positive.   A
Moslem was one who, like Abraham, was *not* one of
the polytheists ; besides this, he was one of those who

feared, *i.e.* were in alarm at the prospect of the Day of Judgment. But as regards other beliefs and practices he was a follower of the Prophet; whatever orders the Prophet issued were incumbent upon him. Those orders, if the Prophet's biography may be trusted, were not always such as approved themselves to the consciences of the Believers; but few of them ventured to disobey, and those who did venture were sternly reproved. Very little was fixed by the time of the Prophet's death; at best some of the Companions were in a position to teach neophytes certain portions of the Koran, but we cannot say how much or what portions. The whole fabric of beliefs and practices, such as fills many a volume, has grown up since that event. The new religion ostensibly took little or nothing over from older systems; with the difficulty which is discussed in the Acts of the Apostles, what authority is to be assigned to the Old Testament, a matter which even the Christianity of our day has at times to face, Islam was never troubled. The attitude of the Jews in Medinah decided the Prophet to break with them entirely, even to the extent of denying the authenticity of their scriptures, and with paganism he had already broken; to Christianity his debt had at no time been considerable. He had, therefore, a *tabula rasa* to write on, and himself used the space at his disposal sparingly. Any further writing upon it might be styled reformation, since that word signifies only altering the shape; and this might be done in many ways.

LECTURE III

FOR the reasons that have been given, the Koran could not by itself serve as a code, or even as a basis of legislation.   And the notion that any documents other than the Koran survived from the time of the Prophet, and could be used to supplement it, was ordinarily ridiculed.   When Ali was asked whether he possessed any information given him by the Prophet other than the Koran, he replied, " Only what is in the Scroll "; this scroll contained the maxim that Believer should not be slain for Unbeliever, but little else.[1]   According to another account, this scroll was kept in the sheath of the Prophet's sword, and Ali's son gave a very different account of its contents.[2] Possibly this scroll is identical with one called the Veracious, which was in the hands of Abdallah, son of 'Amr, the conqueror of Egypt; for which a traditionalist said he would not give one farthing.[3]   A document of somewhat greater importance was the alms-tariff, which was preserved in various forms; the Prophet's biographer gives it in the form of a

---

[1] Umm vii. 292.   [2] *Ibid.*, vi. 3.
[3] Mukhtalif al-Ḥadīth 93.

letter from him to the Yemenite communities; according to others it was a document handed by him to Abu Bakr; according to others it was a revelation, and as such ought to have found a place in the Koran.[1] A similar tariff of compensation for wounds was to be found in another letter of the Prophet,[2] which, however, does not appear to have been preserved. The jurists and traditionalists when they cite these documents cite them by oral tradition. There is no suggestion that the originals were anywhere preserved, although the work from which the references have been taken was not separated from the supposed date of the letters by two centuries.

Since the Prophet described the mission of Jesus as for the purpose of removing some of the restrictions imposed by earlier legislation, it is likely that he meant current practice to continue except where his legislation had abrogated it. So long as this theory could work, there were, then, two sources of law : custom and the Koran. We arrange them in that order, because the matters for which the Koran provided were limited in number. In some of the earliest occurrences of Islam we find custom further defined as the custom whereupon people are agreed rather than that wherein they differ. And to some extent the word " custom " continued to be employed of various institutions which had certainly been taken over by Islam from the earlier practice of Arabia.

The transformation of Arabia into an empire, and the incorporation in Islam of numerous nations and

---

[1] Umm ii. 4.　　　　　[2] *Ibid.*, vii. 295 ; *cf.* 171.

communities with very divergent practice, rendered this earliest theory unworkable; for Arab governors had to be sent out to the provinces, and the need for uniformity made itself felt. Hence a fresh source of law was required, and the Jewish theory suggested an expedient. The Jews have, as is well known, two laws, a Written Law and an Oral Law; the latter has, indeed, for so many centuries been committed to writing that the meaning of the word " oral " in this context is often blurred, and the importance of the distinction forgotten. There is strong reason for believing that the Jewish Oral Law was still oral in the time of the first Caliphs, and even for some time later. Although this Oral Law in the form wherein we possess it consists of lawyers' opinions, in theory it was all delivered to Moses on Sinai. Hence the conjecture lay near that Mohammed had had delivered to him an Oral as well as a Written Law. And the doctrine that this second source of law was not written or to be written lasted for a considerable time. The Prophet is said to have forbidden the writing of it.[1] In some dying injunctions ascribed to a general in the year 82 a man bids his sons *read* the Koran and *teach* the practice.[2] The general who won the throne for the Abbasids is said to have *heard* from his master and have *remembered* traditions.[3] A century later, when at least one corpus of tradition already existed, the formula still is, " I have *read* the Koran and *heard* the tradition ";[4] but in the third century

---

[1] Musnad of Ibn Ḥanbal iii. 26. [2] Ṭabarī ii. 1083.
[3] ii. 1726. [4] iii. 774.

it runs, " I have learned the Koran by heart and written the tradition," *i.e.* copied it down from some teacher's dictation.[1] One of the teachers of the historian Ṭabarī took the trouble to find out whether the pupils had committed to memory what they had written. It was, however, a token of sanctity never to be seen employing written material,[2] other, of course, than the Koran ; but in the case of that work greater merit was acquired by reading than by reciting from memory.[3]

Nor was it difficult to find in the Koran itself evidence for the existence of this second source of law. We repeatedly read of " the Wisdom " as distinguished from the Book. Wisdom besides the Book was given to the Prophets, and was also revealed or sent down to the Moslems.[4] It is true that this Wisdom seems in places to be identified with the Koran, and together with the texts of God it was read in the houses occupied by the Prophet's wives.[5] It might be difficult, even with the most careful consideration of the texts wherein this Wisdom is mentioned, to determine whether the Prophet really thought of it as separate from the Koran ; and on the whole it is probable that he did not really distinguish the two. The Koran is called the Wise Record, and the term *muḥkam* applied to God's revision of the texts points the same way. Still, it was possible to take a different view ; and in the legislation of the end

---

[1] Yākūt vi. 429.
[2] Dhahabī, Ḥuffāẓ i. 303.
[3] Ḳūt al-Ḳulūb i. 61.
[4] ii. 231 ; iii. 75.
[5] xxxiii. 34.

of the second century of Islam we have the definite statement that the Wisdom means ordinances made by the Prophet, yet not embodied in the Koran. And the texts wherein the Moslems are commanded to obey God and obey the Prophet furnished a sound argument for recognising this second source of law— the precedents of the Prophet.

The process whereby "the beaten track,"[1] "precedent," or "custom" comes to mean the precedent set by the Prophet is just traceable in the stories which survive from the early days of Islam, most of them indeed somewhat coloured by later ideas and usage. Sometimes the practice is defined as "past practice"[2] or as "known practice" opposed to innovation,[3] or as good practice opposed to bad practice,[4] or as order opposed to disorder.[5] Sometimes the "practices" are mentioned without further definition,[6] but at times they are ascribed to God,[7] to the Moslems,[8] to Islam,[9] to the first two Caliphs,[10] or to the first two Caliphs and the Prophet;[11] at times they are even mentioned as something over and above the practice of the Prophet.[12] In a manifesto ascribed to Ali, it is asserted that Allah taught the Arabs by Mohammed no fewer than four things—the Book,

---

[1] Ṭabarī ii. 885, 16.   [2] *Ibid.*, i. 3368, 15.

[3] *Ibid.*, i. 2937, 15, 3166, 8, 3298, 9 ; ii. 240, 19 (spurious letter), 984, 14.   *Cf.* 985, 15.

[4] i. 3044, 9.   [5] ii. 455, 14.

[6] i. 3419, 6 ; ii. 1083, 11.

[7] i. 3427, 5.   Aghānī xx. 106 ; Ṭabarī ii. 518, 14 ; ii. 1369, 15.

[8] i. 3132, 4, 3228, 15.   [9] i. 2929, 18.

[10] i. 2976, 10, 3267 ; ii. 1392, 10.   [11] i. 3044, 9.

[12] ii. 1700.

the Wisdom, the Ordinances, and the Practice.[1] In
a solemn address to the founders of the Abbasid
dynasty, the practices are said to be contained in the
Koran.[2] Nevertheless, the " practice of the Prophet "
in these stories is far commoner than any other
phrase. The context in which these expressions are
most frequently used is in reference to the third
Caliph, Othman, whose conduct was supposed to
differ seriously from that of his predecessors: though
the charges formulated against him are always somewhat vague. It seems clear that the second source of
law was not yet anything quite definite, but merely
what was customary, and had the approval of persons
of authority, all of whom presently merged in the
Prophet.

It might seem that this was to assign the Prophet
a function which he expressly disclaimed; for there
is little doubt that he carefully distinguished between
his utterances *ex cathedra* and others. Where he had
a revelation to guide him he was infallible, and his
comrades recognised that infallibility; and indeed
the recognition of any other sort could only be made
at the expense of the Koran. This sort of logic is
found wherever resort is had to oracles; it is a condition of their genuineness and importance that they
should not be capable of explanation as the fruit of
ordinary speculation; hence those who deliver oracles
are madmen, children, jesters, persons to whose re-
flections no value could be attached; indeed, the
tendency to accentuate Mohammed's illiteracy is

[1] i. 3236, 13.   [2] ii. 1961, 8.

evidence of the same theory. When Mohammed ruined a date-crop by strangely and capriciously forbidding artificial fertilisation of the palms, he explained his mistake as due to ignorance; he was not on that occasion delivering a revelation. But it became necessary to supplement the Koranic legislation from his practice, and some evidence of the second function assigned to him, viz. of legislator as well as medium, had to be found in the Koran. The passages then cited for this purpose are those in which the Prophet is said to have been sent "to read unto them Our texts, and to teach them the Book and the Wisdom and to purify them"; and indeed it is stated that " God revealed unto thee the Book and the Wisdom and taught thee what thou hadst not known." Combining these statements with the command in the Koran to obey Allah and to obey the Prophet, the jurists argue that what the Book is to Allah, that is the Wisdom to the Prophet.

Nevertheless it seems clear that is against the intention of the Koran. The Believers are told when they dispute about anything to " refer it to God and the Apostle " (iv. 62), and the Hypocrites are attacked for declining an invitation to refer their differences to what God has revealed and unto the Apostle, and told that they will not count as Believers until they make the Apostle their judge; they are contrasted with those who obey God and the Apostle. The obedience and the belief are the same : they are conferred on the Apostle as the spokesman of God ; the authority and the spokesman cannot be distinguished.

Probably the orthodox opinion is that the Prophet's ordinances are embodiments of the highest wisdom, and therefore deserve the title which is bestowed upon them ; but there are pious authors who admit that this is not necessarily the case. It is a sign of love of the Prophet, says a Ṣūfi author, to prefer his ordinances to the results of reason and intelligence :[1] and this implies that the two may conceivably be at variance. Shāfi'ī confines himself to the arguments that have been quoted ; the injunction in the Koran to obey the Prophet, and the declaration that one who obeys the Prophet thereby obeys God. To the question whether the name " Revelation " may be applied to the Prophet's words, he declines to give an answer.[2]

Professions develop by division of labour, and it must have taken some generations to separate the functions of Koran-reader, Traditionalist, and Jurist. The word which in the Koran means "knowledge" or understanding, but afterwards became the technical term for "law," seems to have specialised somewhat slowly. The second Umayyad Caliph uses it in the sense "acquaintance with the Koran," the only form of book-learning recognised at the time. Ḥusain, he said, had come to grief on the side of his *fiḳh*, which he explained to mean that he had forgotten a text in the sacred volume wherein it is stated that God assigns the sovereignty to whom He will.[3] It is rather surprising to find a man sign

---

[1] Ḳūt al-Ḳulūb ii. 85. [2] Umm vii. 271.
[3] Ṭabarī ii. 381, 2.

himself "the jurist" as early as the year 66, and one is inclined to fancy that the title was given him by some later scribe.[1] The "jurist" was still, as Ṭabarī somewhere describes him, the pious man who performs devotional exercises in the mosque, and gives legal opinions when asked.[2] The home of this knowledge, *i.e.* what the Prophet had said and done, especially in matters which bore any relation to law, was naturally Medinah, where he had first assumed the rôle of ruler and judge ; and indeed the people of Medinah had a high appreciation of their acquaintance with this subject, and demanded that their governors should consult them about all cases which came before them—a demand which no other city appears to have made.[3] This demand, indeed, some of the governors conceded of their own accord.[4] The people of Medinah were long recognised as the most thorough students of the subject and the most careful to supplement omissions.[5] We are told that the year 98 was called the year of the Jurists, because the majority of the Medinese jurists died in it. At a later period Kufah obtained university rank in this subject.[6] Before the close of the Umayyad period every governor was supposed to possess some legal training.[7]

That the Medinese jurists obtained something more from the Jews than the mere idea of an Oral

---

[1] Sha'bī, Ṭabarī ii. 613, 5.   [2] ii. 881 ; 564, 16.

[3] ii. 1452.   [4] ii. 1183.

[5] Shāfi'ī, Umm vii. 242.   [6] Ṭabarī ii. 1620.

[7] ii. 1837, 126 A.H.

Law is very likely; in one or two cases the terminology of the Arabic jurisprudence can be traced to the language of the Mishnah. It is, however, characteristic of Moslem studies that they take very little from outside; they develop on independent lines. And the fact that Medinah is the home of Moslem jurisprudence of itself indicates that the amount borrowed from non-Jewish sources is likely to have been exceedingly small; for Medinah was purely Arabian and Jewish, and the level of cultivation among the inhabitants decidedly lower than that of Meccah. As questions arose, the persons to whom they were referred were residents in Medinah, notably the widows of the Prophet, because they naturally had most acquaintance with the Prophet's life. There is no evidence that Roman Law penetrated into this primitive city; when the residents were asked for legal opinions, they had to rely on their memories, their intelligence, or, at best, local talent. The Jews who had adopted Islam were far better equipped than their fellow-citizens for practical jurisprudence, although there is no evidence that their law was already codified; they had, however, at their disposal the results of reflection and experience such as could be applied in many cases. And the general method of jurisprudence, principles for reconciling conflicting passages in the sacred book, and deducing unforeseen consequences, had undoubtedly been elaborated by the Jews many centuries before the rise of Islam.

This, then, appears to have been the genesis of

the second source of Law, which has provided the
Moslems with their main occupation. The very
name "beaten track" is clearly more suitable to
general *custom* than to the precedents set by a single
individual; the other name "talk," "narrative"
might conceivably be regarded as a translation of the
Jewish phrase *mishnah*, but it may have arisen in-
dependently, in any case in some antithesis with the
written code. At the earliest period of the civil wars
it appears to have been recognised that conceivably
neither the Koran nor any other source of law
provided for every emergency; "This is a new affair,"
says a Companion; "It never happened before this
day, so that there could be a Koranic revelation about
it, or a precedent in the conduct of the Prophet";[1]
"They gave judgment without any convincing plea
or any past precedent," complains another.[2] Like
other general negations, the former of these propositions was hazardous, since methodical examination
of the Koran might find much whose presence was
unsuspected by the superficial student, whereas the
Prophet might have provided for the emergency by
some precept which had escaped the speaker's notice.
And indeed it was presently discovered that the
Prophet had foretold the future even to the extent
of naming sects which came into existence long after
his death.

When this point was granted, viz. that the
practice of the Prophet was no less binding on
mankind than the legislation of the Koran, and that

---

[1] Ṭabarī i. 3166, 8.   [2] *Ibid.*, 3368, 14.

both were equally revelation dictated by God, but merely differed in form—the one being put by God in His own language, the other communicated to the Prophet to deliver as he chose—there still remained a question as to the relation between the two forms of Law : was the Prophet's practice merely comment upon the Koran, *i.e.* limiting and explaining, or was it supplementary as giving rules on subjects which the Koran did not itself treat? Some certainly asserted that it was all of it of the former sort; there was no ruling of the Prophet on any subject of which the basis was not to be found in the Koran. But this proposition could not be maintained without difficulty.

Between the two forms of revelation there was, however, one difference. It was maintained that though the Koran could abrogate itself, it could not be abrogated by the Prophet's practice. The arguments for this doctrine are Koranic texts; they are taken from verses wherein God claims the right to alter the Koran, and asserts that when any text is abrogated, one that is better or at least as good is substituted. From this it is reasonable to infer that the substitute is invariably to be got from the Koran itself, and not from the Prophet's contributions. One other text that is quoted is less convincing; it is where the Unbelievers request the Prophet to produce a Koran different from this, and he replies that he cannot possibly alter it *proprio motu*,[1] for if the *sunnah* (practice) be revelation, such an alteration could not be called *proprio motu*.

[1] x. 16.

Shāfi'ī quite correctly reasons that just as the Koran can only be abrogated by itself, so the *sunnah* can only be abrogated by itself. He has, however, to resort to the assumption that we possess both the Koran and the *sunnah* in their entirety, since otherwise there would be a chance that the abrogated verse might in certain cases be preserved, and the abrogating lost ; and similarly that the abrogated practice had been remembered, but not the abrogating.

One of the most important functions of the *sunnah* is clearly to settle between conflicting texts which abrogate the other ; for, as we have seen, the evident intention of the compiler of the Koran was to leave this matter absolutely undecided ; all suspicion of chronological arrangement had to be avoided. In the cases to which reference was made above, it was clear that no one could say which passage was the earlier. And we can scarcely be wrong in inferring that even at this early period of Islamic jurisprudence it was acknowledged that on many subjects the revealed law was inconsistent.

The confession that parts of the most precise legislation in the Koran had been abrogated by other parts must have been a trying admission to make, but there was no way of avoiding it. In Surah ii. 176 the dying Moslem is enjoined to bequeath his property to his parents and near relatives. In Surah iv. certain fixed portions are assigned by the law to these relatives ; clearly the property cannot both be bequeathed and divided by the state. But perhaps he has the right to bequeath the whole ? The tradition is here cited that according to the Prophet the right of legacy is restricted to one-third.   Or perhaps the text of Surah ii. may be still valid, as meaning that legacies may be made *only* to relations.   Here we have an ingenious argument based on a story that some Moslem whose whole property consisted of six slaves manumitted them by will. The Prophet cancelled this arrangement, and manumitted two by lot; the rest were to be assigned in accordance with the law of Surah iv.   But since the Prophet permitted the legacy of one-third of the estate and the beneficiaries were the legatee's slaves, and no Arab has a kinsman for his slave, it follows that the restriction of legacies to kinsmen has no existence.   There is therefore nothing for it but to declare the text of Surah ii. abrogated by that of Surah iv.

The question of the treatment of adulteresses is even more serious.   In Surah iv., which is called the Surah of Women, and contains a great deal of precise legislation, the punishment assigned is imprisonment for life.   In Surah xxiv., of which the date can be accurately fixed, since it deals with the affair of 'Ā'ishah, which again is connected with a particular campaign, the punishment assigned is a hundred stripes.   But the tradition is that the Prophet administered the stripes to the adulterer, ordered him to be banished for a year, and ordered the adulteress to be stoned.   If, then, the last was the practice to be followed, not only was one text of the Koran abrogated by another, but both were abrogated by practice.   Some attempt might indeed be made to accommodate the second text and the practice to differing conditions, but the text of the Surah of Women had clearly to be disregarded. What is probably the case is, that the Prophet's treatment of the offence grew less instead of more barbarous, and that his final views were represented by Surah iv.; but the practice of exacting the worst penalty was too deeply sanctioned by custom to be overridden even by Koranic texts. The affair of 'Ā'ishah had become so famous that the slandering of women was regarded as a deadly sin, which even the earliest Islamic creed was said to have especially prohibited, and the evidence on which a charge of adultery could be established was practically of a kind which could never be produced.

The inherent weaknesses of this second source of law are, of course, two. In the first place, we look in vain for evidence that exhaustive records of the Prophet's sayings and doings were kept. Shāfi'ī himself accounts for differences of opinion between the " learned " on the ground that some tradition may have escaped them; had they known more, they would have been guided by that superior knowledge.[1] In the second place, the memories of those who transmitted traditions were weak, and the author of the code himself repeatedly confesses that he has forgotten the name of some intermediary or other;[2] and at times that he has forgotten the exact words, though he believes that he has reproduced the sense correctly.[3] The jurists of the preceding generations could not rely on

---

[1] Umm iv. 171.   [2] *Ibid.*, vi. 3 ; *cf.* iv. 71.   [3] vi. 172.

their memories with any greater certainty; Sufyān Thaurī forgot the name of an intermediary on whose authority a tradition was quoted; one of his class reminded him, but this was apparently not quite satisfactory.[1] The possibility of error and ignorance is allowed in the case of contemporaries of the Prophet.[2] And, indeed, Shāfi'ī is said to have made a general confession that there was no one whom the practice of the Prophet did not escape,[3] though he assumes that somewhere in the Moslem world this knowledge is preserved.[4] Hence when the second source of law is considered, there is generally the double doubt whether there was any precedent or maxim really going back to the Prophet, and if there was, whether it was his final opinion on the subject. And the omission of a name in the chain of authorities naturally invalidates the whole.

Further, in the case of the Prophet's practice there was the same difficulty as was found in the Koran, viz. that his rulings varied from time to time, and chronology had to decide which ruling was to be followed. Sometimes, indeed, the chronology gave a satisfactory solution. Thus on the question of the attitude to be adopted in prayer, whether if the leader be prevented by infirmity from standing upright the followers also should refrain from standing, there were reports of two occasions on which the Prophet set precedents; one of these happened to be on the occasion of the Prophet's last illness: clearly this

[1] Umm vii. 41.

[2] *Ibid.*, vi. 163.

[3] Yāḳūt vi. 387.

[4] Umm vii. 265.

had to be followed, since there could not have been a later occasion.

Besides this, there was at times conflict between the Prophet's maxims and his ascertained practice: on such occasions Shāfi'ī apparently holds that the maxim is to be followed. A serious case in which he is confronted with this difficulty is that of murder by a Moslem of a Jew or Christian: the historical evidence appeared to show that the Prophet and some of his successors ordered the same treatment as would have been adopted if the Christian had been the murderer; the latter was handed over to the relatives of the murdered man, to kill, forgive, or compel to pay blood-money as they chose; and, indeed, where the relatives of the murdered man expressed their desire to forgive the offence, the Caliph took pains to see that this was not due to intimidation. On the other hand, the Prophet was credited with the maxim, " Believer shall not be slain for Unbeliever," delivered on a variety of occasions. The jurist, then, adopts this maxim as regulating procedure, and has to reject the historical traditions as weak, or suppose that the Prophet's successors were mistaken.[1] And in other cases where the decisions ascribed to the foremost of the Prophet's Companions differ from the Prophet's practice or from his maxims, it is agreed that the former are not deserving of consideration. Where there is a known ruling of the Prophet, no one else has anything to say. Useful as this maxim is, it has the difficulty that these same persons are also the

---

[1] *Cf.* Ṭabarī ii. 83.

most trustworthy witnesses of what the Prophet said
or did; and their fallibility to a certain extent dis-
credits the whole system of legislating by the Prophet's
precedents.

Occasionally it is in our power to show that the
traditions which form the basis of the codes are legal
fictions. The historian Ṭabarī tells us the practice of
obtaining redress for murders by unknown persons
by administering oaths wholesale was an innovation
of the year 30—a score of years after the Prophet's
death;[1] the jurist Shāfi‘ī bases it on an anecdote of the
Prophet's procedure, which indeed is on other grounds
clearly apocryphal.[2] The practice of administering
stripes for wine-drinking is said by the historian to have
been introduced by general consent in the time of the
third Caliph;[3] the jurist also finds a precedent in the
Prophet's practice. And in general the history of
the jurists differs widely from that of the historians.
European critics are inclined to attach more weight to
the statements of the historians. It is painful to find
one of the founders of the science of law confessing that
he had pleaded the genuineness of a document which
he secretly suspected of being a forgery, and therefore
declined actually to attest; the result, which was the
serious one of inducing a man of ability and influence
to join the party of the unscrupulous adventurer
Mukhtār, being equally attained. In any other case,
then, this person's inclinations may have caused him
to play fast and loose with his critical conscience.[4]

1 Ṭabarī i. 2842.   2 Umm vi. 78.

3 Ṭabarī i. 3028.   4 Sha‘bī.

That the whole system of the Oral Law did not escape ridicule in certain quarters is natural. There were the objections to which allusion has been made, the fact that the traditionalists themselves confessed to lapses of memory, so that one of these persons is represented as quoting someone else for an assertion which he himself had made: " I was told by Munḳidh, who heard it from *me*, who heard it from Ayyūb " ;[1] and the fact that there were contradictory traditions dealing with the same matters. Then the content of many traditions was clearly fabulous and calculated to bring the system into ridicule, *e.g.* that the Prophet said the thickness of an Unbeliever's skin in hell will be forty divine cubits, or that the wind is not to be abused because it is the breath of God. Further, the traditionalists were taunted with being ignorant and often unable to compose correct Arabic. It could be replied that a man might be a good traditionalist without being a good grammarian ; that the collecting of traditions of various degrees of probability was for the purpose of criticising them and selecting those of which the genuineness stood proper tests ; and the charge of stupidity could also be rebutted. The fact, however, was that this collecting of traditions had been the result of the needs felt by the community, and it would seem that those who ostensibly rejected the process were content to profit by the results. Hence the similarity between the codes compiled by the different sects of Islam shows that the basic traditions were in

---

[1] Mukhtalif al-Ḥadīth 92.

reality recognised though there might be reasons for professedly ascribing the laws to a different origin, *e.g.* the esoteric knowledge communicated by the Prophet to members of his family.

What must be said of the jurists and traditionalists is, that whatever the value of their second source of law, they spared no pains in endeavouring to recover it. In order to find out the true amount of the *jizyah* or tribute exacted from Jews and Christians in the Yemen under the Prophet's regulation, Shāfi'ī travelled over the whole of that country and asked for information in every province.[1] In order to discover the true theory of pious benefactions, he consulted many of the descendants of the Refugees and Helpers in the sacred cities.[2] He consulted more than one member of the family of Omar and of the family of Ali about practice.[3] What he did in his time was doubtless done by others before his time, and it is partly due to the rise of this source of law that posterity knows so much about the Companions of the Prophet, each one of whom was a sort of oracle.

In order to compile a code of law on so strange a foundation as casual observation of what one man had said or done, research had indeed to be indefatigably carried on; and since it was impossible to leave questions unanswered, much had to be accepted on very imperfect attestation. Shāfi'ī has a paragraph in which he compares the evidence required for legislation with that required in a law court, and he admits that the latter is stricter in many particulars.

[1] Umm iv. 101.   [2] *Ibid.*, iii. 276.   [3] *Ibid.*, iii. 281.

For a tradition he is satisfied with the evidence of one man or one woman: in court he requires more. He will take hearsay evidence for a tradition, if the reporter is of good character; but in court he requires firsthand knowledge. In the case of conflicting traditions he will accept *one*, using as criterion its agreement with some other source of law: but he cannot deal in the same way with conflicting affidavits. On the other hand, he claims to demand in the reporter of a tradition a higher degree of intelligence than he would demand from a witness, because it is sufficient in the case of a tradition if the sense be retained though the words may be altered; but it requires a certain degree of intelligence to know when an alteration in the diction will not affect the sense. Whereas, then, in court he is prepared to assume that credible witnesses guarantee the credibility of their authorities, in the case of traditions he does not take this for granted, but has to institute an inquiry into each link of the chain.

Shāfi'ī's argument for receiving a single attestation in the case of a tradition, whereas the law courts are not satisfied with less than a double attestation, is highly ingenious. One of his points is that in the case of a tradition the attitude of the reporter is purely objective; he cannot be suspected of partisanship in matters which affect all Moslems alike. It was, however, clear that the whole theory of traditional law must break down if a single attestation was excluded. For, in numerous cases, the rulings of the Prophet were supposed to take, or actually did take, the form of messages communicated through a messenger or delivered to an individual. Many a piece of information about his conduct was communicated to the world by *one* of his wives. And, indeed, the biography of the Prophet offered numerous occasions on which matters of the highest importance had been communicated in this way. When the congregation was praying at Kuba, a messenger arrived from the Prophet telling them that in accordance with a revelation which has just descended, they are to reverse the direction of prayer; the attestation of a single messenger satisfies them, and they reverse the direction in consequence. The command to spill all spirituous liquors was communicated by single messengers and was immediately obeyed. Indeed, on certain occasions, when it would have been easy for the Prophet to have sent a number of messengers at once, he was satisfied with sending one and unquestionably expected that the message would be obeyed.

Shāfi'ī further points out that the individuals sent with messages were persons who were known to the individuals or communities to whom the missives were directed, and who therefore were in a position analogous to that of reporters of traditions to Moslem communities of a later age.

Any precedent, however authoritative the person responsible for it, had to give way before a tradition of the Prophet. Where a tradition could be cited, the common sense of the individual judge had to give way. One saintly follower of the Prophet,

Abu'l-Dardā, declared he could not live in a country where the sovereign set his own opinion against the practice of the Prophet; the question being whether an object made of a precious metal might be sold for more than its intrinsic value. Common sense would seem to be in favour of the workmanship, etc., being assigned some value, but the Prophet's dictum was against it. In discussing the credibility of witnesses, Shāfi'ī is satisfied that no Jew or Christian is a credible witness; his sole argument is that the Koran charges these sects with corrupting the text of their sacred books; into the justice of that charge it is not his business to inquire, neither does he consider whether, if it be true, it falls on all existing members of those communities, or whether the culprits were persons in a bygone age, whose work it is not now possible to undo. He does not even take notice of the fact that the Koran itself distinguishes between different members of those communities, allowing that there are honest as well as dishonest persons among them. And, as will be seen, he has some real difficulties to face, but a little experience might have shown him that if it was the desire of the judges to arrive at the truth, this ruling of his barred and bolted many of the avenues.

One principle which is too deeply ingrained in these works ever to be forgotten is that only oral tradition counts; written documents must be cited from memory, not from the text. Traditions are to be condemned merely on the ground that they are taken from documents;[1] and as we have seen, "the

---

[1] Mukhtalif al-Ḥadīth 93.

Veracious Scroll," said to be in the possession of a Companion, was rated very low. A man who procures an old letter learns it by heart, so as not to forget it, he does not apparently *copy* it.[1] Letters of early Caliphs or other persons of importance are then regularly cited in this way; and when Shāfiʻī cites a deed of gift by Ali to some tribe, he cites it as he heard it read out to him by the Governor of Medinah, not as he read it.[2] Hence no attempt appears to have been made to secure the preservation of the originals of these valuable documents, about which the handwriting expert might perhaps occasionally have had something to say. The only theory which explains this strange delusion appears to be that the Koran tolerated no literature besides itself. Somewhat similarly the supposed Letter of the Christian Saviour to Abgar, King of Edessa, which is cited in letter-form by Eusebius, is given as oral tradition in the Syriac account, which is not much later, for fear that this letter should demand admission into the Gospel; and, as we have seen, a place in the Koran seems to have been claimed for the tariff of alms, which was contained in a letter of the Prophet. And since the Prophet's letters had been drawn up by his scribes, there might have been some difficulty about stopping this source of additions to the Koran if the perpetuation of any collection of letters had been tolerated.

Hence we read of a practice whereby people took down traditions, learned them by heart, and then

[1] Ṭabarī ii. 502, 3.
[2] Umm iii. 279; letters cited, vi. 125; vii. 135, 291, 293.

discarded what they had written.   The cases wherein a permanent record was preserved somewhere seem isolated; there is an interesting story that a copy of the poems composed by the Prophet's court-poet, Ḥassān Ibn Thābit, was preserved in Medinah, and regularly renewed when the writing showed signs of evanescing; but written bodies of tradition appear to be mentioned only after the founding of Baghdad. The vast journeys taken by traditionalists were therefore futile, since they only collected matter which might easily have been communicated by one man or learned from books; for, from the very formulæ wherewith the traditions are introduced, it is evident that the teachers claim to be nothing more than intermediaries; if what they communicated was original, it was false.   They were not like the teachers of the true pronunciation or even the true interpretation of the Koran, who might well have matter to communicate which was either their own property or else only communicable orally.   One dated copy of a collection of traditions, guarded like the poems of Ḥassān at Medinah, would have been better evidence of authenticity that any number of " paths." We can only then suppose that the fear lest the Koran might be superseded was what delayed the process of committing this matter permanently to parchment or papyrus; and when at last that step had been taken, the notion that no written copy was authoritative had become too firmly implanted to be uprooted.   It must, however, be added that the forgery of letters appears to have been exceedingly common,[1] and the repeated exposure of such fabrications may have brought the written word into discredit.

Just as we find misquotations in the New Testament and the Jewish tradition, one name being substituted for another, or non-Biblical matter being called Biblical, so the Koran was occasionally misquoted, as, *e.g.*, by Manṣūr in his letter to the Alid pretender, or even some secular author confused with the divine author to whom that work was ascribed. The human memory is everywhere untrustworthy ; only, such occasional misquotation hurts no one when there is a text whereby it can be remedied. In the case of the Tradition there was no check, and if even a professional student of tradition like Shāfiʻī frequently confesses that his memory is at a loss, we need have no confidence that the memory of any other reporter was better. Sometimes the ascription of a saying could be put right ; Abū Ṭālib points out that one which was ordinarily ascribed to the Prophet really belonged to the Ṣūfi Sahl al-Tustarī of the third century. Some of the Prophet's sayings were referred to earlier revelations, and can indeed be identified in the Bible or Apocrypha. The principle of jurisprudence whereby in civil suits the plaintiff must produce evidence, whereas all that can be demanded of the defendant is an oath, is sometimes referred to Omar, at other times to the Prophet, whereas it really comes from the Jewish Mishnah. The study, therefore, of the development

---

[1] Ṭabarī ii. 1312, 1870, 1882, etc.

of jurisprudence is exceedingly complicated ; for the maxims ascribed to the Prophet seem in numerous cases to be little more than a summary of existing practice, and yet there is no doubt that these maxims when formulated and so ascribed had a great effect on subsequent legislation.

Still, codification of the accumulated mass of practice must at an early period have become a crying need ; and unofficial codes are likely to have been compiled and even issued before any received the sanction of the central authority. As early as the year 128 we read of an official appointing a committee of pious men to make a collection of *sunan* or approved practices and *siyar* rules of conduct, which were then to be written out by his scribe.[1] Afterwards a document called the *sīrah* of Ibn Suraij, or " line of conduct," was actually circulated.[2] Before this time the building up of a system of jurisprudence had been facilitated by the classification of subjects, under which precedents and maxims could be collected ; this appears to have been done during the first century in Medinah, where the study of Islamic law started, and where the author of the code which dominates in the Maghrib passed his life. As in other cases, seven names during this period became classical in connection with the study, though not all agreed about the names to be placed in the list.

The studies of the Medinese jurists of the first century are no longer in existence ; the great

---

[1] Ṭabarī ii. 1918.   [2] *Ibid.*, 1921.

Pandects which were compiled by the doctors of the second century assume the work of their predecessors and are based upon them. It is fortunate for those who are interested in the historical development of Moslem law that the works of several of the founders of law-schools are still extant. In that of Shāfiʻī we find that the study has not yet quite emerged from the controversial and dialogue form. Shāfiʻī records the discussions in which he took the leading part, the arguments adduced by his opponents as well as his own, and so takes the reader into his workshop. We learn from these discussions that the collection and criticism of tradition had already been highly developed; the disputants are already familiar with the traditions quoted under each heading, and with the chief inferences drawn from them; some canons for ranging the traditions in order of credibility have already been formulated, and the great principle that the sole source of law is the Prophet in one capacity or another is acknowledged. When Shāfiʻī challenges his opponent to reject the principle, the audience permit no dispute on the point. But further, we find that grammatical and lexicographical studies of which the purpose is fixing the meaning of the Prophet's utterances have already gone a long way. And still more we are struck with the subtlety of the disputants, and their skill in constructing imaginary cases. Probably it is less subtle than the discussions recorded in the Jewish Gemara, but it has the merit of being far more practical and generally intelligible.

It was in the course of these discussions, then, that the systems of law got built up. The audience decide which of the disputants has the better of the argument; and the anxiety of each to defend his position leads to the enucleation of various principles, and in general the fixing of the Sunnah, and some sort of rating of the traditionalists at various values. No amount of acuteness, however, can compensate for the fundamental weakness of the system: the possibility that any text of the Koran may have been abrogated, and the liability of any tradition to be questioned. Most of the discussions illustrate this. We may refer again to the question whether the murder of a Jew or Christian by a Moslem is punishable with death; the Koran throws little light on this matter, except that it quotes as a precept given to Moses the maxim " a life for a life." Only it does not follow that this precept was to be taken on by the new religion: it may have been abrogated by it as many other ordinances were abrogated. Then we come to the practice of the Prophet: one tradition is to the effect that one 'Amr Ibn Umayyah was killed by the Prophet for a murder of this kind; but to this there is the reply that this could not have been, since 'Amr Ibn Umayyah survived the Prophet. The conduct of the Prophet's Companions in similar cases was no less ambiguous: Omar wrote that the murderer should be executed, and then wrote to countermand the order. Othman ordered an execution, but was dissuaded by his colleagues. No less difference prevails as to the amount of the blood-money due. Either it is the same as due for a Moslem, or it is half, or it is about a third.

In spite, therefore, of the keenest desire on these persons' part to abide by the Scripture and the Tradition to the exclusion of their private predilections, they had after all to be guided by the latter ; those who wished to uphold the privileges of Islam took one line, those who thought rather of the welfare of the whole community took another. The leading jurists even employ the formula "I like," "I dislike," thereby implying that they are settling things according to their predilections : though doubtless these were what they supposed to be most agreeable to the system of the Koran. In the *Mudawwanāt* ascribed to Mālik in ordinary cases the reporter merely gives the question which he had addressed to the hearer of Mālik as to Mālik's handling of some question, and then reports the answer : which at times is to the effect that Mālik was not known to have expressed an opinion on it : but more often is an actual opinion without quotation of the arguments whereby Mālik would have defended it. Hence the charge made against the Jews in the Koran of having taken their Rabbis as gods in addition to God, in the sense that they assigned the Rabbinical legislation a value not second to that of the Scripture, might towards the end of the second century have been brought against the Moslems also : the words of the great jurists became a source of law, whereas legislation was a privilege of God Almighty.

Having adopted this curious source of law, Shāfiʿī proceeds to deduce principles with great acuteness. The Prophet is supposed to have acknowledged that when cases were pleaded before him it was possible that one of the litigants might be a better pleader than the other, and he, the Prophet, might in consequence give an erroneous verdict: but he warned such pleaders that anything which was in consequence wrongly assigned them was a strip of Hell Fire, whence they had best not avail themselves thereof. From this tradition a whole series of inferences are drawn. One is that it is the duty of the judge to follow the evidence without endeavouring to go beyond it; another, that the judge's ruling does not alter the rights and wrongs of the case; a third, that it is lawful for a citizen to set aside the ruling of a judge when it is in his favour; a fourth, that the divine vengeance is threatened to those who take moneys assigned to them from the public treasury which are not their due.

The second of these inferences is of some importance, as it precludes the employment of precedents, except where they are taken from the practice of saints of the first order. Shāfiʿī indeed distinguishes two cases: one in which a sentence is found afterwards to contradict either Scripture or Tradition; in such a case a succeeding judge has the right to reverse it. Another is the case in which there is no question of Scripture or Tradition, but only of analogy, in which different opinions might reasonably be held. Supposing that after taking one view a judge changes his mind, he is not to reverse his decision nor should a succeeding judge reverse it, though in future cases he might follow the view which had finally commended itself.

The view of Omar in a letter of instructions, which is probably apocryphal, was that any judgment might be rescinded when the judge discovered that there was a preferable opinion to that which he had at first adopted.

If one compares the volumes of Shāfiʻī and Mālik with the Mishnah and Gemara, the comparison is favourable to the Moslem jurists from several points of view. First of these is the speed with which the science of jurisprudence was evolved; two centuries had not elapsed from the Migration before the Moslems had a system based on principles, which, if doubtfully wise, at any rate are as wise as those followed by the Jewish lawyers. And if there be any merit in excogitating questions of casuistry, the Moslem can conceive situations as unlikely to arise as any imagined by the Jew. Shāfiʻī describes the case of a Moslem aiming at a Christian and the latter being converted before the arrow hits him, or of a slave being manumitted in the interval that elapses between the direction of the arrow and its piercing the victim.[1] It does not seem that the Moslems ever made the mistake of thinking jurisprudence easy, and supposing that lawyers quibbled out of pure malignity; the Moslem authors certainly did not aspire to rise above their source, the Prophet, but

[1] Umm vi. 33 end.

they took endless pains to ascertain what views he had held, and to work these out to their proper consequences. Although not many Greek books can have been rendered into Arabic before the end of the second century, Shāfi'ī displays some acquaintance with the Aristotelian logic, and is clear about the meaning of the words "genus" and "species." His arguments from analogy are also highly ingenious. The Prophet forbade the keeping of dogs, except for certain necessary purposes; hence Shāfi'ī argues that there is no property in dogs, and that if a man kill a dog his owner has no right to compensation. Why not, asks the opponent, if the dog be kept for one of these useful purposes? The reply is that the licence is limited to the owner; the case which may be compared is that of carrion which under necessity may be eaten; it is clear, however, that no one who burned such carrion would be liable to pay damages: and the case of the dog is comparable to that of the carrion, as being permanently in a state of prohibition, from which it can be temporarily exempted, but which does not become property thereby.

A study of the great Pandects on which the Mālikite and Shāfi'ite systems are based suggests that any influence which earlier systems of jurisprudence may have exercised on those of Islam must be looked for at the commencement, and no later. Some few technical terms appear to be borrowed from Christian or Jewish systems, but the bulk of the development is independent, and the possibility of foreign ideas being adopted seems to be excluded.

The whole is dominated by the rough-and-ready nature of the Prophet's utterances; and though we may refuse to believe the authenticity of a large proportion of the traditions on which the reasoning is based, it seems difficult to put the invention of them later than the first century: if the maxims were not the hasty and capricious utterances of the Prophet, they were formulated by persons no more capable of improvisation. If we wish to know what is the age at which human beings become responsible agents, it is settled by the story of a man being rejected as a soldier at the age of fourteen, but admitted in the following year; what we may be clear about is that this story settled the question, and it makes little difference whether there was any truth in it. The growth of this subject, then, resembles the growth of Arabic grammar. A few ideas, the rudiments of grammatical categories, were got from the Greeks through the intermediation of the Syrians; but the rest of the fabric is Islamic, built up by observation of the usage of the Koran, and to some extent that of the language actually spoken in Arabia. In both cases the fabric is so vast that these foundation stones are all but concealed.

LECTURE IV

THE Prophet's chief experiment in constructive politics was the institution of tolerated cults—a sort of caste-system, since by this arrangement whole groups of the population were to enjoy a special status. Certain religious communities were to be allowed to remain outside the Moslem brotherhood, unmolested on condition of their paying tribute; only various disabilities were imposed upon them. This institution differed from other caste-systems in one notable matter: it was in the competence of any member of the tolerated cults at any moment to join the dominant community, by pronouncing the Moslem creed. In other countries transference from one caste to a higher was an impossibility, the castes being supposed to be an ordinance of nature which no human power could alter; or could only be brought about by the special favour of the sovereign, usually as a reward for eminent service. The experiment was started so late in the Prophet's career that the resulting problems scarcely made themselves felt during his lifetime; he apparently desired that so long as tribute was paid, there should be as little interference as possible with Jews and Christians; the incorporation within the Islamic empire of whole countries in which the population was Christian commenced after his death. Proselytism from Christianity to Islam scarcely took place—at any rate on a noticeable scale—before the expansion of the latter under the first Caliphs.

So long as all that Islam demanded from members of tolerated cults was tribute, it might be argued that their condition compared favourably with that of the Moslems. For the difference between the tribute paid by the Christians and the alms paid by Moslems might seem to be purely a difference in name. It was the claim for alms which determined the Arabs to revolt after the Prophet's death. The difference in name was, however, considerable; the alms constituted an honourable payment, purifying the Believer who contributed it; whereas the tribute was a form of humiliation, which might even be regarded as a brand of slavery.[1] Acceptance of Islam, on the other hand, involved a whole number of onerous obligations : various religious exercises, some of them—*e.g.* the fasting-month—by no means acceptable; and, besides, compulsory service in the field, which, as we learn from the Koran itself, was at times found irksome, notwithstanding the prospects of booty and Paradise. Although the historical evolution of the Islamic caste-system was by no means favourable to the subject caste, some of the traces of this original condition survived. Exemption from military ser-

---

[1] Shāfi'ī, Umm vii. 292.

vice and from the burdensome ceremonies of Islam aided the tolerated communities in a variety of ways, and counteracted some of the effects of humiliation and oppression.

Unforeseen problems arose, which had to be settled so far as possible by the maxims of the Koran. Certain texts made it clear that the family tie was cancelled by the religious change; the Jew or Christian who adopted Islam had stepped out of the family to which he formerly belonged, and had formed a new connection; the rights and duties which had formerly belonged to him had all lapsed. He then forfeited any claim to inheritance which his membership of a family had given him, and also deprived that family of all right to inherit from him. The doctrine that there was no inheritance between members of different religious communities came to be asserted with such strictness that some jurists extended it to Islamic and even to Jewish and Christian sects.

To some, however, this seemed to be dealing justice too evenly between Believers and Unbelievers; it was argued that where conversion to the dominant community took place it should only confer advantages and should occasion no detriment; let the convert retain his claims to inheritance if he had any, only let his unbelieving relatives be excluded from any share in his estate. Provision had also to be made for the rare case wherein the transference took place in the opposite direction, *i.e.* from Islam to Judaism or Christianity; such a pervert doubtless forfeited his life, but did his believing family thereby lose all claim to what they might otherwise expect to be theirs? The ordinary administrator would settle this question in the interest of the Moslem community, and could argue that in certain other cases Islam scored both ways, or at any rate made no pretence of treating the subject cults as equal to itself. The most familiar example is the case of women: a Moslem man may marry a Christian or Jewish woman, but a Moslem woman may not become the wife of any but a Moslem man. We are apt, when we eulogise Islam for its unification of races, to forget that this unification is somewhat one-sided. The system regularly demands that the mate of a Moslem woman must be her equal, but makes no similar claim for the Moslem man—in whose case the word "mate" is scarcely suitable. The needs of the treasury were against retaining the Moslem convert's right to an inheritance from his former family; the state was surer of its right when the inheritance remained with Jews or Christians. And the case of the pervert from Islam was rather academical than practical. The estimable Ali, it was said, when ordering the execution of a pervert, probably on a historic occasion, had assigned his estate to his Moslem relatives. Shāfiʻī, insisting on the maxim that there is no inheritance between members of different creeds, decided that by perversion a man deprived his Moslem relatives of their right to his estate. A theory which had been devised for dealing with such cases—viz. that the death of the pervert may be presumed, because any Moslem who found him would have the right to kill him, whence his estates might be divided on perversion as they would be after death—is rejected on the ground that there is always the chance of reconversion, which would restore to the man his rights as a Moslem. Nevertheless, though Shāfi'ī neglects the interests of the pervert's family, he does not neglect those of the state. If the pervert be out of reach, his goods may be considered spoils of war, and assigned to the treasury for the community.

Several questions which arose from the recognition of tolerated cults were connected with the poll-tax. Although the Moslem conquerors seized some of the best provinces of the Byzantine empire, they recognised the independence of the latter, and repeatedly treated with it; there was ordinarily no question of enforcing on it the payment of the tribute which was enforced on the Christian residents of the provinces which had been conquered. How far was this state of things in accordance with the doctrine that Islam was to triumph over all other cults, and that the realisation of that triumph was the duty of the Moslems? The orthodox explanation was that a respite had been granted to the Greek empire because Heraclius had treated with respect the letter of the Prophet which bade him adopt Islam; unlike the Persian monarch who had torn the Prophet's letter to pieces, Heraclius had preserved the despatch sent him in musk. The reception of the missive by the Greek emperor is indeed a very favourite subject of myths on the part of the Prophet's biographers, who regularly represent the emperor's conduct in a favourable light; indeed, suppose him to have been converted, but to have had his hand forced by the ecclesiastics. Heraclius thus secured the continuance of his empire; only, in order that the Meccan merchants who had traded with Syria might not be damnified, the divine providence had ordained that Syria should be withdrawn from Byzantine rule.

It must, however, be emphasised that the duty of the Moslem sovereign to reduce all non-Moslem states to subjection by force of arms never actually lapsed, though circumstances may have rendered it difficult or even impossible to execute. The fact of an independent Christian state existing—or indeed of such a state existing belonging to any other religious community—is a sufficient ground for an attack. And the court historian of the Ottomans, who wrote with the express object of glorifying the first eight Sultans of that dynasty, makes it the great merit of Othman, the founder, that he attacked the Christian strongholds in Asia Minor and so increased the territory of Islam; there were prosperous cities in his neighbourhood, which owing to the weakness of Byzantium and the rival empire could not defend themselves against aggression, and pay with employment was wanted for the refugees from the relics of the Seljuk empire; Othman, according to this chronicler, who took care to say nothing which his masters would not approve, attacked these cities, and forced the inhabitants either to adopt Islam or to pay tribute; the old industries were ruined, and the churches with few exceptions turned into mosques. We are not here concerned with the question whether other religious chiefs adopted the same view of their duties towards their neighbours, but merely with the question whether this was or was not the view taken by orthodox Islam.

In the second place, the word "the Book," occurring in the text which enjoins warring on those who had been given it until they paid tribute, admits of various interpretations. And indeed the phrase "who have been given the Book" need not imply that they still possessed it; hence Ali is quoted for the assertion that the Persian Mazdians had once possessed a revealed book, which had been taken away from them owing to the crime of a certain king. On the other hand, the tense of the words "who have been given the Book" confines the permission of tribute in lieu of Islam to those who had received the Book before the revelation of the Koran; whence only those communities which had followed one of these systems before that memorable date can claim exemption from death or conversion. And since the text speaks of fighting with these sectarians till they pay tribute, it follows that only the fighters among them have to pay it: women and children are excluded. The theory that only those communities have a right to toleration who never possessed a better revelation is carried out to its logical consequence. Thus an Arab Jew or Christian is not to have the rights of other Jews and Christians, on the ground that the Arabs originally belonged to the Ḥanifite faith and abandoned it; they are therefore in the position of renegades.

For the same reason conversion from one tolerated cult to another is not permitted, since the principle which underlies toleration is continuity; and indeed in the instructions which the Prophet is supposed to have given his earliest lieutenants, the wording of the order was to the effect that no Jew or Christian should be forced to abandon the faith wherein he had been born. But when once the continuity has been snapped, the Jew or Christian may be supposed to have returned to natural religion; if, therefore, he joins a non-Moslem community, it may be argued that he is in the position of a pervert. This principle occasioned some difficulty when missions began to work among the Christian populations of the Ottoman empire; when the Foreign Office in the year 1840 demanded a firman for the erection of a missionary Protestant church in Jerusalem, the reply was at first offered that the Christian subjects of the Porte were forbidden by law to pass from one community to another.[1]

The different Christian sects were locally separated in the Moslem empire; and since they were placed under responsible heads who were in direct communication with the Moslem officials, it is probable that the difficulties which arose from this provision were ordinarily small. It is noteworthy that fresh Jewish sects sprang up under Islamic rule, but fresh Christian sects appear not to have started in these

---

[1] Engelhardt, *Tanzimāt,* i. 61.

regions. The reason is that the Moslem conquest of Mesopotamia meant the renaissance of Jewish literature, but the practical death of the Christian literature of the East.

An important feature in the condition of the tolerated cults according to the Islamic system was that the members were not to bear arms, or take part in the wars of the community. Nevertheless, Shāfi'ī reserves to the sovereign the right to employ these persons as soldiers, supposing that the Prophet's refusal to allow the Jews to fight on his side at Badr was cancelled by a later precedent: the precedent which he cites is absolutely fictitious and a gross anachronism; two years after Badr, he states, the Prophet employed Jewish auxiliaries of the Banu Kainuka against Khaibar. However, if there be any truth in the Prophet's biography, the Banu Kainuka were banished shortly after Badr, having escaped with difficulty from a general massacre; and the attack on Khaibar was five years after Badr. Later exponents of Shāfi'ī's code make it a condition of the employment of Unbelievers as troops that the sovereign has convinced himself of their loyalty, and that they do not outnumber the Believers in the army. Mālik appears to have confined the possibility of employing Unbelievers in campaigns to work that was not, strictly speaking, fighting—as sappers or engineers.[1] He is unaware of any precedent whereby the Prophet's practice with regard to Badr was annulled; indeed, he asserts that when Medinah was

---

[1] Mudawwanāt iii. 40.

itself attacked in the following year he declined to avail himself of the help of the Jewish residents. The assignation of the spoil in the case of raids occupies a large space in Moslem law, and such a share so clearly falls to the fighter in virtue of his being a Moslem that there are difficulties about assigning it to an Unbeliever; Shāfiʻī therefore prefers that when such persons are employed they should be treated as hirelings.[1]

The introduction of weapons of precision must have made a great difference in the question of bearing arms, and the meaning of the word "disarm" have come to be far more definite than when personal strength counted for everything in warfare. Until the attempt to introduce universal service in the Ottoman empire, when Christians fought side by side with Moslems, it would appear that the former were regularly members of independent communities; it is highly improbable that the loyalty of the Christians resident within the Islamic empires could be trusted, and this, as we have seen, is a condition of their employment. Even when Islamic cities were undergoing siege, it is probable that the Christian population could not be trusted to take part in the defence; but our records seem singularly silent on this subject. The fact appears to be, that after some futile attempts at rising in the provinces which contained Christian communities, the latter gave up the idea of forcible resistance to oppression as hopeless; at times they welcomed invaders, and

---

[1] Umm iv. 177.

on certain occasions indulged in short-lived triumphs when those invaders had been successful. The jurists, however, forbid them to possess arms, and about this there would seem to be general agreement : the abandonment of arms is one of the conditions to be demanded when they capitulate. It is rather curious that in the Prophet's biography the Jews figure as dealers in arms and armour just as they do in the mediæval England of Scott. Apparently they could be trusted not to use them effectively.

Another matter, for which, however, some guidance might be found in the old Roman law, was the extent to which the Moslem government should interfere with the practices of the protected communities. Shāfi'ī poses the interesting question whether if a protected community were raided by a foreign power, which proceeded to prevent it from exercising its rights—*i.e.* drinking wine and eating pork—it would be the duty of the Moslem powers to rescue these clients, and so enable them to go back to practices which the law of the Moslems condemned : and he decides that this would be the Moslem government's duty. He holds also that the contract whereby the Jews and Christians are protected involves in it obedience on the part of the members of these communities to their own magistrates : these magistrates are as much officers of the ruling powers as are the Moslem magistrates. If a dispute between members of these communities be referred to the Moslem magistrate, he is not obliged to decide it ; if the parties refuse to submit to the ruling of their own magistrate, they may be charged with violation of their contract with the Moslems; only, if the Moslem magistrate choose to decide the case, then he must decide it according to Moslem law. And that Moslem law precludes the acceptance of any but Moslem witnesses.

This last seems a harsh enactment, and one system admits the evidence of the tolerated cults against each other; but difficulties followed from accepting any other doctrine. For if witnesses be accepted from any other community than the Moslem, they must submit to analogous tests; and then, just as the most pious Moslem is the most credible witness, so the most pious Jew or Christian will be the most credible among his co-religionists: which leads to the strange result that the persons most averse from Islam will be those to whose witness Islam attaches value. Dating by the Christian Easter was forbidden on the ground that its calculation was made by Christians; it is not clear whether Shāfi'ī was aware that the dating had anything to do with the moon.[1] Moreover, the law of Islam only accepts the evidence of freemen; if it were to admit that of Jews or Christians it would be placing the free Unbeliever above the believing slave; which is expressly against the valuation of the Koran.[2] And, indeed, the fact that the free Moslem is not necessarily a qualified witness without attestation to his character makes this question of employing witnesses of other communities exceedingly difficult. For the character

[1] Umm iii. 85.   [2] ii. 221.

of a witness in the case of a Moslem means his observation of Islamic ordinances.

Still, it was impossible to reject all non-Moslem attestations, and an oath may be exacted from a Jew or a Christian. An interesting case of such exaction is where a Jew or Christian has sold a Moslem wine and declares that he was not aware that such sale was forbidden. The magistrate is to demand an oath, and if the dealer takes it he is acquitted.[1] Different views were held as to the formula of the oath to be employed. Some said it was to be by Allah only; others allowed an oath by the Law or the Gospel. And some, in order to ensure greater sanctity, maintained that it should be taken in some place which the member of the tolerated cult held sacred.

It was, of course, impossible for the government to avoid the exercise of all jurisdiction in the case of members of tolerated cults. To a certain extent Islamic law had to be imposed upon them, and that distinction between civil and criminal law which the Moslem jurists are on the whole justly charged with ignoring forces its way to the front. Mālik is asked why he enforces on a Christian the Moslem penalty (handcutting) when he is found guilty of stealing, but does not enforce it in the case of adultery, when the crime is committed by non-Moslems: his reply is that the former only is injurious to the community. In the main, then, the principle was to leave these communities to their own practices

[1] Umm iv. 126.

when the life and property of the public were not thereby endangered, but to interfere when such danger was involved; the Moslem government does not, however, undertake to protect the *honour* of the subject sects, and only interferes to protect it when Moslem interests are involved. An exceptional case of interference with custom is its refusal to tolerate the incestuous marriages with which the Mazdians were charged. It acknowledges property in wine and swine, when Christians are the possessors, but does not acknowledge it when they are in the possession of Moslems. This ruling, though apparently in accordance with justice, was not approved by many pious sovereigns; in Egyptian history we read not unfrequently of general raids on the wine stores and wholesale destruction of their contents. The excuse in such cases was doubtless that Moslems could not be prevented from procuring them when stores existed in their neighbourhood.

For cases of murder wherein members of tolerated communities were involved assimilation of some sort to Moslem law was necessary, and complications arose from the differences of social organisation which resulted. A murder, by the law of the Koran, was regarded as an injury to the family which thereby lost a member, and which might either retaliate by taking the life of the murderer, or might instead take a sum of money or its equivalent in goods; a difficulty being that the whole family of the murdered man had to agree before execution could take place, and this, according to one system, involved waiting until any minors in the dead man's family had grown up.[1]   Shāfi'ī regards all non-Moslem sects as one community for this purpose; idolaters are to be allowed to retaliate on Jews, and conversely.   He also gives these sects the right of mutual inheritance, which, as has been seen, some jurists disapproved.

With regard to the relative value of Moslem and Unbelieving lives, it would appear that the view of the earlier period was more equitable than that of the later; as has been seen, a number of traditions are cited according to which such convinced and even fanatical Moslems as Omar and Ali, when a Moslem had murdered a Christian, handed the murderer over to the family of the murdered man, or else themselves ordered his execution; and a tradition even ascribed an act of strict justice of this sort to the Prophet himself.   Other traditions were cited to show that in the earliest period the blood-money was the same for all denominations; and both these theories were accepted by Abu Ḥanīfah, whose code is official in the Ottoman empire.   Shāfi'ī, however, while demanding the execution of an Unbeliever for the murder of a Moslem,[2] emphasises the maxim, 'Believer is not to be slain for Unbeliever," and assesses the blood-money for a Jew or Christian at one-third that due for a Moslem, while he fixes that for a Mazdian at one-fifth.   The Moslem murderer of an Unbeliever is, however, according to him, to be punished, but not excessively, whether the punishment take the form of stripes or of imprisonment.

---

[1] Umm vii. 136.   [2] *Ibid.*, vi. 33.

The former should not be numerous ; and the period of imprisonment ought not to be longer than a year.

The maxim quoted is, of course, ascribed to the Prophet, though different views were held as to the occasion whereon he delivered it. In mitigation of it, it must be observed that murder was not regarded as a criminal offence, and the state provided no executioner for such cases : the executioner was to be a member of the injured family, who had to obtain their authorisation before he could proceed to retaliate : and it might well be undesirable to permit the execution of a member of the ruling caste by a tributary in any circumstances. To us it seems extraordinary that whereas in the case of some other crimes commutation of punishment is not permitted, in this case it is.

Even in modern times there has been grave difficulty in forcing Islamic sovereigns to introduce equality between their subjects in this matter. It was asserted that the first time when any independent Moslem community had executed Moslems for the murder of Christians was after the lamentable massacres of Adana ; and it will be remembered that English journalists dreaded the results of the execution of Butrus Pasha's murderer on the ground that in Egypt the execution of a Moslem for the murder of a Christian was contrary to the law. One would fancy that this was a case for the application of the maxim *mala consuetudo abolenda est*. There would seem to be a probability that cases must have occurred before the Adana affair in which such executions were ordered by Moslem sovereigns, for the death-punishment was inflicted in all Mohammedan states with great readiness and capriciously. The maxim of the Prophet which has been quoted ordinarily regulated procedure.

The law-books assume that both Jews and Christians recognise the institution of slavery no less than Moslems; and indeed they could scarcely do otherwise, living in a civilisation that was based on this institution. It is, however, a legal principle that a Moslem may not be slave to a member of a tolerated cult; he may only be the slave of another Moslem. So soon, therefore, as a slave adopts Islam, it is the duty of the governor to enforce his sale by his Christian or Jewish master; just as, if a Christian or Jewish wife adopts Islam, her husband is compelled to divorce her, or else to adopt the religion himself. Cases of difficulty arise, when the woman is converted during the husband's absence; the governor is instructed to see whether the absence is likely to be long or short; and to delay the divorce or enforce it accordingly. Mālik forbade a Moslem to hire himself out to a Christian in any capacity, *e.g.* as agricultural labourer.[1] He forbade him to let his house to anyone who intended to use it for the sale of wine or pork.

A peculiar case of disability is recorded in the legislation of the pious Caliph Omar II., who enacted that the tax on trade should in the case of Christian or Jewish traders be double of what was paid by Moslems.

---

[1] Mudawwanāt xi. 75, 159.

It would seem that the relations between Moslems and Christians steadily deteriorated, doubtless owing to the natural effect of communities with different rights and of different status living side by side. During the earliest period the relations would seem to have been friendly and at times even affectionate. The persons who are accused of doing mischief in the land are said to raid the protected cults.[1] Governors who are sent out to take charge of provinces are commanded to deal justly with the people of the *dhimmah*,[2] and Ali in his dying injunctions to his sons insists upon this.[3]

A scene is described by Ṭabarī which occurred after the defeat by one of Ali's generals of a body of rebels who had been joined by their Christian neighbours. In accordance with the Caliph's orders the Moslem captives are released, but the Christians with their families are to be led off. Their Moslem allies accompany them until the general bids them return; compelled to part, they embrace, and the scene was the most affecting which its narrator had ever witnessed. Presently these Christian captives find a Moslem chief who redeems them and gives them their liberty at tremendous cost; in the attempt to pay this in full he afterwards loses his liberty. It is true that Ali's general in his despatch states that it was his intention to give these Christians a lesson and remind them that they are humble and degraded; but it would appear that

---

[1] Ṭabarī i. 2922, 7 ; 2993, 21 ; 3303, 15.
[2] 3247, 1 ; 3430, 14.　　　　　　　　　[3] 3463, 5.

this doctrine had not yet sunk in the Moslem mind.[1]

In the references to the condition of the Christian subjects of the Moslem empire for the rest of the Umayyad period we find evidence of a condition of things which is on the whole satisfactory. The authorities regularly regard the defence of the Christian populations as their duty.[2] The usurper Yazīd, who defended his usurpation by the iniquities of his predecessor, in his manifesto declares that he means to watch over the interests of these subjects, and do nothing which will tend to drive them from their homes or reduce their birth-rate.[3] A son of the Caliph Hishām (who died in 125) complained to his father that a Christian employé had struck his slave ; the Caliph told him that he must bring an action in the ordinary way, and when another slave of the prince took the law into his own hands, he was punished by the sovereign.[4] Deserting soldiers are charged with desiring to pillage the Christian communities which they are likely to pass on their homeward journey, an act which the authorities do not countenance.[5] The accusation which meets us so frequently at later times of undue favour being shown to Christians who usurp the public offices scarcely is found in Umayyad times. Possibly the idea of working the bureaux themselves was not yet quite familiar to the Moslems. Some fanatics in the

----

[1] Ṭabarī i. 3438, 19.
[2] ii. 934.
[3] ii. 1831.
[4] ii. 1731.
[5] ii. 1873.

year 119 are represented as charging a somewhat notorious governor with destroying mosques to build churches and synagogues, and giving Moslem women to men of the tolerated sects, but our historian does not confirm the accusation.[1]

From the third century onwards we find repeated allusions to the Ordinance of Omar, or general regulation of the conduct to be observed by members of subject cults, on pain of losing their treaty rights. The account of the ordinance is correctly given by Sir William Muir: "The dress of both sexes and of their slaves must be distinguished by broad stripes of yellow ; they were forbidden to appear on horseback, and if they rode a mule or an ass, the stirrups must be of wood and the saddle known by knobs of the same material. Their graves must be level with the ground, and the mark of the devil placed on the lintel of their doors. Their children must [not] be taught by Moslem masters. Besides the existing churches spared at the conquest, no new building must be erected for the purpose of worship ; no cross must remain in view outside nor any hammer be struck. They must refrain from processions in the streets at Easter and other solemn seasons." Further, it would seem that the churches already in their possession must not be repaired, and that they must be employed in no government office, wherein Moslems would be under their orders. The nature of the saddle permitted was such as to suggest humiliation ; it was used for parading persons who had incurred

[1] Ṭabarī ii. 1623.

some serious punishment about the streets.[1] The intention of the regulation about the dress was to render it impossible to mistake one of them, even from a distance, for a Moslem.

It can scarcely be said that these ordinances are contrary to the spirit of Islam in the second century, if the great jurists are authoritative interpreters of the latter. " Mālik was asked concerning certain persons who went raiding, and disembarked in Cyprus, where they proceeded to buy sheep, honey, and butter, and payed for these articles with dinars and dirhems ; Mālik disapproved. He further said to us of his own initiative : ' I strongly object to coins which contain the mention of God and His Book being taken and given to one that is unclean. I disapprove most strongly of such a practice.' I asked him whether we might make purchases with dirhems and dinars of traders who disembarked on our coast, or of members of the tolerated cults. He replied that he disapproved. He was asked whether money might be changed by changers in Moslem markets who belonged to these cults. He replied that he disapproved."[2]

According to the same jurist the capitulation of the subject cults involves their paying a poll-tax and a land-tax. Supposing such a land-owner sells his land to a Moslem, he, the Christian or Jewish owner, will continue to pay the land-tax, because this was one of the conditions of his capitulation ; and he is not even allowed to contract out. Supposing, how-

---

[1] Ṭabarī ii. 192, 7 ; 1653, 6.   [2] Mudawwanāt x. 102.

ever, that the Christian owner adopts Islam, then he ceases to pay either poll-tax or land-tax.

The enactment that Jews and Christians may not ride horses, or use a saddle resembling that of a horse, is found in the code of Abu Ḥanīfah, who is ordinarily the most tolerant of the four. It is agreed that both men and women belonging to these communities must distinguish themselves in their dress from the Moslems, and also that their houses must be distinguished by a mark, doubtless no honourable one.

The pious Caliph Omar II., in a rescript to a governor, told him to destroy no churches which came within the contract, but also to let no new ones be built.[1] The question whether new churches may be built is discussed by Mālik, who replies in the negative. His pupil, however, makes a distinction between cases. Suppose the Christians are left in possession of a village, having agreed to pay tribute : in such a case, since the land theoretically still belongs to them, there can be no objection to their doing what they like in this matter. Where, however, the chief community is Moslem, or where a city has been built by Moslems, as, *e.g.*, Fusṭāṭ, Baṣrah, or Kufah, they should not be permitted to build. The same code forbids a Moslem to sell his house to a Christian who has any intention of turning it into a church ; to let his house for similar use ; to sell an animal to the member of a non-Moslem community who is likely to use it for a sacrifice ; or to hire out a beast to be ridden at one of their feasts.[2]

---

[1] Ṭabarī ii. 1372.   [2] Mudawwanāt xi. 66.

The distinction between the case in which a community dwelling in a place was originally Christian, and that of Christian residents on what was from the first Moslem territory, is also emphasised by Shāfiʿī.[1] He is particularly concerned with the outward display and conduct of the religious ceremonies belonging to these communities. These may be permitted in the former case, if the original contract involved such permission; but are prohibited in the latter. If the Christians assemble at all for religious worship, it must be in private, and their voices must not be raised. Abu Hanīfah gives permission for the repair of such churches as need it, but it is probable that this was not permitted by the other jurists.

The question to whom the ordinance goes back does not concern us; what is certain is that it was frequently enforced. The historian Tabarī was born in 224 or 225 A.H.; in his Chronicle he records the events of the year 235, and even produces a copy of a proclamation issued by the Caliph of the time, al-Mutawakkil. This letter contains the strictest regulations concerning the dress which the Christians are to wear, and the nature of the saddles. In Tabarī's account the Caliph also commanded that all new churches (*i.e.* such as had been built since the capitulation of the community) should be destroyed, that the tenth part of their quarters should be seized, and a mosque be built upon it if it were of sufficient space, otherwise be left vacant; wooden demons should be nailed to their doors in

---

[1] iv. 126.

order to distinguish a Christian house from a Moslem house; they were to be expelled from all offices in which they had any control over Moslems, their children were to be turned out of all Moslem schools and Moslems were not to give them instruction, their graves were to be levelled with the soil in order that they should not resemble the Moslem graves.[1]

Ṭabarī is, as we have seen, recording an affair that took place when he was ten years old or more. In the year 239, when he was fourteen years old, Mutawakkil introduced even severer measures, forbidding them to ride horses; they were only to be allowed asses or mules.

Ṭabarī records these enactments with no comment, and without adducing any justification for them.

And what we gather from the chronicles is that the Ordinance of Omar was at any time liable to be enforced, and the members of the tolerated communities were never safe from it. It was not found possible to keep them permanently out of the bureaux; for the public business had somehow to be transacted, and few Moslems were qualified to transact it, while little confidence was reposed in those who were qualified. The disabilities of the subject communities in a way ensured their fidelity. But their promotion to high office provoked jealousy, and their employers could not always protect them, unwilling as they doubtless often were to get the business of the bureaux into disorder. When therefore the cry was raised that the Ordinances of Omar had been violated,

---

[1] Ṭabarī iii. 1390.

the jurists naturally went with the people in the matter, and it was difficult for the sovereign to refuse to listen.   In the year 500 a vizier is cashiered and restored to office on condition that he is to employ none but Moslems.   In the year 529 a Christian vizier is appointed by the Egyptian Caliph ; he fills his offices with Armenians, and according to the historian oppresses and humiliates the Moslems. Popular discontent finds expression in an organised revolt; the vizier is compelled to flee from Cairo, and finally enters a monastery ; vengeance is dealt to the Armenians whom he had favoured.   We are not ordinarily in a position to assess the rights and wrongs in these cases ; sometimes, as in the last case, the Moslem historians assert that there was provocation for the attack, sometimes they make no such suggestion.   What we infer is that the Ordinance of Omar was frequently enforced, and was at any time likely to be.

A story is told at length by Makrīzī in his history of the year 700 (1301 A.D.), made accessible by M. Quatremère in his French translation.   A vizier of the Maghribi Sultan arrives in Egypt, and sees a man on horseback, surrounded by numerous mendicants, whom he asks his attendants to remove from his path. The vizier, learning that this horseman was a Christian, was deeply wounded.   He went to find the Emirs Baibars and Selar, told them what he had seen, expressed his displeasure, shed copious tears, and spoke of the Christians with extreme contempt.   " How," said he, " can you hope for the favour of heaven, when

Christians in your country ride on horseback, wear white turbans, humiliate the Moslems, and make them walk in their trains?" He expressed his disapproval in strong terms, dilated on the obligation imposed on the members of the government to keep these tributaries down and compel them to adopt another costume.

The Emirs bring the matter before the Sultan, and an edict is promulgated enforcing the " Ordinance of Omar." The Christians and Jews were summarily dismissed from all government offices; they were forbidden to ride horses or even mules. The Christians tried hard to bribe the officials to get some relaxation of these orders; but the Emir Baibars "displayed laudable zeal and extreme firmness in maintaining what had been resolved." The populace, encouraged by a legal decision, rushed upon the churches and synagogues and demolished them. All houses occupied by Jews or Christians in Alexandria which outtopped Moslem houses were pulled down.

The theory that no new churches might be built and no old ones repaired, and the ordinance that no church might be higher than a mosque, were perpetual sources of chicanery. In the chronicles of Egypt under the Mamlukes references to this matter are exceedingly common. In 846 A.H. it is discovered that a Melkite church and certain other churches in Cairo had been repaired; the authorities close them in order that the licence for their repair should be exhibited. An order bearing date 734 is produced, and the matter is referred to the Shāfiʻite and Mālikite

Kadis. In the meantime some trouble occurs with the Jews and a council of state is held, after which it is decided that the old contract of Omar is to be renewed according to which no church, synagogue, or convent is to be repaired or renewed. If any attempt at repairing one be made, the whole building is to be destroyed. In 851 it is discovered that in spite of this ordinance repairs have been effected in a Melkite church, and the Sultan in consequence orders its destruction.

Clearly it was useless to allow them the churches at all unless repairs were permitted. It would, moreover, appear that in this case permission for modest restoration had been obtained from one of the deputies of the Shāfi'ite Kadi. Some praying at the tomb of a saint was required before the order could be procured for the destruction of the church, which was carried out by the high officers of the state deputed for that purpose by the Sultan.

In the year 849 a charge is brought before the Sultan that on Mount Sinai there are six churches which exceed in height the old mosque that is continuous with the convent. The question whether these churches are not also posterior to the capitulations is also raised. A commission is sent to inquire, and in consequence the churches are destroyed. Similarly, in 850 a complaint is brought that a Melkite church is higher than a neighbouring mosque, and the Sultan in consequence orders its destruction.

Nor do we find that Christians have any fixity of

tenure. Ibn Iyās records that in the year 759 it was discovered that there were in Egypt 25,000 feddans appropriated to churches and monasteries: doubtless the gifts of a long series of benefactors. The finance minister before whom this matter was brought was deeply chagrined; he consulted the Sultan, who issued an order that all this land should be withdrawn from the possession of the Christians and distributed among the military chiefs as additional fiefs. He then issued a further order for a general destruction of churches and monasteries. The historian does not even suggest that there was any provocation justifying this measure, except the fact that the Christians were discovered to be in possession of the property. Similarly, in recording the life of the Sultan Chakmak, the historian records that he once grew angry with the Christians and ordered a number of their churches to be destroyed.

It is, of course, possible to assert that the series of massacres and plunderings which have marked Moslem rule over Christians had always some occasion which was not merely the difference of belief. In the history of Egypt under the Mamlukes we find the Christians constantly charged with incendiarism; and, in consequence, during the reign of Baibars the whole community ran the risk of being committed to the flames. But, indeed, to suppose that in Moslem countries Christians would not undergo persecution for their faith is to take a view of human nature which is incompatible with facts. The governments were ordinarily tyrannical and extortionate; there was constant misery caused by usurpers and invaders ; in such cases the resentment which cannot with safety be directed against the government finds its vent, with the approval of the government, in attacks upon the defenceless alien.

Mr Pickthall speaks of poor Moslems and Christians chaffing each other on the subject of their religions, but that has at all times been a dangerous game ; for the poor are those who care most. The poor in Egypt or Syria are the scrupulous worshippers, who fast throughout Ramaḍān and say their five daily orisons ; comfort brings indifference. When in the year 284 A.H. there was a rumour that a Christian servant of the Sultan's Christian physician had abused the Prophet, the mob of a whole quarter of Baghdad was in an uproar ; the object of the authorities appears to have been to quiet them.[1]

It certainly appears from Arabic literature that the Moslems regularly were invited to take part in the Christian festivals and habitually enjoyed this privilege ;[2] we do not—to the best of my belief—read often of return invitations ; and, indeed, the chief festivals of Islam are too definitely connected with the system, too exclusively Islamic, to render the presence of one who was not of the fold any more welcome on these occasions than at the service of the mosque. And although the Christian festivals were on the whole an occasion for the establishment or

---

[1] Ṭabarī iii. 2162.

[2] Maṣāri' al-'Usshāḳ 382. Ibn Athīr x. 166. Sibṭ Ibn al-Ta'āwīdhī, index.

maintenance of friendly relations between the communities, the Moslem government occasionally went to the length of forcibly suppressing them on the ground that they led to riot and debauchery. In the year 759 A.H., under Sultan Ḥasan, the feast of the 8th of Bashans, called the feast of the Martyr, whereon a ceremony connected with the rising of the Nile was celebrated and had been from time immemorial, was forcibly suppressed ; the church which contained the relic which was employed was demolished and the relic itself burned. The excuse was that the feast, which was celebrated by the erection of booths along the Nile, and wherein the whole Egyptian population took part, led to drunkenness and debauchery. In the year 787 A.H. Sultan Barḳūḳ suppressed the Coptic New Year's Day ; this apparently was a feast which bore some resemblance to our Boxing Day, in that *bakhshish* could be demanded with threats, and the persons who refused to bestow were liable to insult ; the bazaars and markets were closed, and anyone walking in the streets, however eminent, might be squirted or pelted with rotten eggs. The festival resembled a Bank Holiday in various ways ; among them, that there was often much drunkenness and brawling. In the main, however, according to the description which the historian gives, it was more likely to lead to good feeling between the different classes of the population than anything else.

The history of Christian communities under Moslem rule cannot be adequately written; the members of those communities had no opportunity of describing their condition safely, and the Moslems naturally devote little space to their concerns. Generally speaking, they seem to have been regarded as certain old Greek and Roman sages regarded women: as a necessary annoyance. Owing to their being unarmed their prosperity was always hazardous; and though it is true that this was the case with all the subjects of a despotic state under an irresponsible ruler, the non-Moslem population was at the mercy of the mob as well as of the sovereign; they were likely scapegoats whenever there was distress, and even in the best governed countries periods of distress frequently arise. Owing to the unequal assessment of their rights as compared with those of the Moslems, wrongs committed by them against Moslems were likely to meet with terrible punishment, whereas wrongs committed upon them were likely to go unpunished. The terrible reprisals occasionally taken by the Christians when they momentarily got the upper hand, as when the Mongols obtained possession of Damascus, show that the relations between the lower classes of the two communities were constantly strained. Writers of whom better things might be expected often report with evident delight excesses committed against them, and the name " enemy of Allah " is applied to them indiscriminately without any sense of impropriety in the expression.

It is probable that the attitude of the sovereigns and of the educated classes was on the whole friendly and respectful. It is rather interesting that in the records which we have of discussions in the fourth century of Islam, to which period the best Arabic literature on the whole belongs, the audience, who naturally belong to a superior class, do not approve of fanatical vituperation; they treat the Christian representatives of science and philosophy as deserving of esteem. And it would seem that the sovereigns had good grounds for preferring to employ them in various offices of trust in lieu of employing their own co-religionists. A Fatimid Caliph wishes to poison his son; he applies to his Jewish physician; the man replies that this does not come within the range of his science, which extends no further than the very mildest of potions and lotions; the Moslem physician when summoned immediately does what is required. The Christian or Jewish minister was aware that any exercise of power on his part would be fiercely resented by the Moslems who were under his control; the paraphernalia of office would, in his case, be regarded as intolerable arrogance, and impious presumption, likely to bring down the wrath of the Divine Being on the whole community; any severe measure against a delinquent Moslem would be treated as intentional humiliation of Islam. The culprit would have the sympathy of the religious world, and his cause might be pleaded in the mosques. Indeed this fact was discovered very early in Moslem history, and is stated by the Umayyad governor 'Ubaidallah b. Ziyād quite naïvely. He employed Persian tax-collectors because if an Arab tax-collector defalcated, he had the sympathy of his clan; if a Persian did, the governor could punish him without danger.[1] Hence the Christian or Jewish minister had the very strongest reasons for displaying loyalty to his chief; for his safety depended entirely on his doing so, since the highest place would never be given to one of his persuasion. It is true that loyalty to a sovereign might incur the vengeance of the next usurper who displaced him; but at times these persons could be got to see that such loyalty was a valuable quality which would be of service to them, when the permanent official came into their employ, and were disposed to reward it even when it had been used against themselves.

The literature, which is not, like the *Arabian Nights*, pure fiction, is full of tales of terrible oppression. A form of passion which is nameless would appear at one time to have been as familiar among Moslems as of old among Hellenes. Christian lads seem often to have been the unhappy objects of this passion. A story is told us by the biographer Yāḳūt of a young monk of Edessa or Urfah who had the misfortune to attract the fancy of one Saʻd the copyist. The visits and attentions of this Moslem became so offensive that the monks had to put a stop to them. Thereupon this personage pined away, and was finally found dead outside the monastery wall. The Moslem population declared that the monks had killed him, and the governor proposed to execute and burn the young monk who had occasioned the disaster, and scourge his colleagues. They finally got off by paying a sum of 100,000 dirhems.[2]

---

[1] Ṭabarī ii. 458.   [2] *Dictionary of Learned Men,* ii. 26.

Forcible conversions to Islam appear to be against the express orders of the Prophet, who in a letter ascribed to him by his biographer insisted that neither Jew nor Christian should be disturbed in his religion so long as he paid the tax. Such events, however, have taken place, and indeed wholesale on certain occasions; the tolerated cults were not only penalised by the mad Ḥakim, but the Al-mohades in Africa at one time destroyed all places of worship belonging to Jews and Christians, and those members of these cults who declined to change had to escape by exile if they wished to preserve their lives. At certain periods conversion was actually discouraged by the maintenance of the poll-tax upon the converts; in express defiance of the spirit of Islam, but the loss to the revenue could not otherwise be met. The disabilities which attached to the tolerated cults, however, had their natural result in bringing over to the dominant community those who were either careless about the faith which they had inherited, or whose career lay in the service of the state, and who found themselves unable to discharge that service efficiently so long as their religious profession excluded them from all those functions for which the profession of Islam was required. Hence the chronicles record numerous cases of men who had obtained some promotion in the service of the state by their talents yielding to persuasion on the part of the sovereign to accept Islam in order to win their way to yet higher honours. Persons who quarrelled with their co-religionists, or who regarded themselves as the victims of oppression among them, had in conversion to Islam a fairly easy mode of obtaining redress.   It would seem, however, that the relations between such converts and their former associates at times remained friendly, the imperious necessity of the step taken being often, or at any rate sometimes, recognised.

Moslem authorities delight in recording conversions effected by other causes than imperial influence or command or the prospect of promotion ; nor need we doubt that cases of conversion out of conviction or temporary enthusiasm at times occurred.   A writer who takes great pains to give chains of authorities for even trivial incidents records how a Christian, whose name he gives, heard a pious Moslem at night reciting the text of the Koran wherein it is asserted that all who are in heaven and earth offer Islam to God ; the words thrilled the hearer so powerfully that he fainted, and presently came to be admitted into the Moslem fold.[1]   We read of a bookseller who adopted Islam because he found that the copies of their sacred books made by Jews and Christians were careless and contained many various readings, whereas those made by Moslems were absolutely identical and scrupulously correct.   At times Jews or Christians who wished to pursue studies qualifying them for the medical profession joined Islam because the leading teacher happened to be a Moslem and declined to admit any but co-religionists to his courses.

Since in all these cases the motive could only work

----

[1] Maṣāri‘ al-‘Usshāk 144.

one way, *i.e.* in the direction of bringing proselytes over to Islam, whereas no proselytism could take place in the opposite direction, it is a marvel to all who have considered Eastern Christianity and its circumstances since the Islamic conquests that it should have survived at all; and the experimental study of religion is compelled to acknowledge and encouraged to find reasons for this vitality which is in such striking contrast to the weakness of classical paganism, to which there was said Die! and it died.

LECTURE V

ALTHOUGH the Moslems were frequently invited to sacrifice life and goods in the cause of their religion, asceticism is scarcely a Koranic aspiration; since its Paradise offers among other delights pure water, clarified honey, milk that has not turned sour, and wine that is a pleasure to drink, administered by fair cupbearers,[1] it evidently does not despise these good things; and there are texts showing a proper appreciation for all forms of wealth, including jewellery and fine clothes, which indeed are to form part of the joys of Paradise, where the blest are to wear silk garments and be adorned with gold bracelets and pearls.[2]   Hence, when in the Prophet's biography we find persons of acknowledged sanctity anxious to possess themselves of such treasures, and disputes arising over the allotment of booty, there was nothing in such conduct at all contrary to the Moslems' profession.   And this appreciation of the value of wealth rendered the mission far less disastrous than it might otherwise have been; the wanton destructiveness which often accompanies such enterprises was kept

---

[1] xxxvii. 43; xlvii. 17.   [2] xxxv. 34; xliv. 33.

in check. It is highly creditable to the Prophet himself that he devised a system whereby the Moslems should be able to live by a tax on other communities, whom therefore they would have an interest in preserving. And it was afterwards found that his practice in the matter of destroying the property of enemies was regulated by economical doctrine. Where he felt sure of ultimate victory, he spared the property as much as possible, since it would ultimately become the possession of the Moslems, its owners being either slaughtered or enslaved; the latter name being employed in this context of the tolerated communities. The later legislation therefore recommended the same course where there was a reasonable prospect of success.[1]

The Companions of the Prophet, then, for the most part amassed wealth, and the transformation of Meccah and Medinah from obscure settlements into the religious and political capitals of a mighty empire was sufficient of itself to enrich those who possessed land or houses in either, owing to what is now called unearned increment. A Meccan house which had been purchased in pagan days for a skin of wine was afterwards sold for 60,000 dirhems—and this was far below its value.[2] The value of the estates possessed by the Prophet's cousin Zubair was found to be 50,200,000 dirhems,[3] and fabulous figures are quoted for other Companions of the Prophet.[4] Huge fortunes were built up out of the plunder which

---

[1] Shāfiʿī, Umm vii. 324.   [2] Jāḥiz, Bayan ii. 108.
[3] Bokhari, ed. Krehl, ii. 281.   [4] Jamharat al-Amthāl 58.

reached Medinah in camel-loads from Persia, Syria, and Egypt. We are told, and may well believe, that the Arabs had at first little knowledge of the value attaching to the objects which they looted so easily; but better knowledge was speedily acquired, and the mere size of the establishments maintained by the Islamic heroes indicates the magnitude of the fortunes which they amassed. In the year 68 we read of a noble Moslem possessing a thousand slaves;[1] and a son of the pious Omar, himself reverenced for his sanctity, manumitted the same number[2] before his death.

Among the persons with whom the Prophet had from the first to deal were those who had no aspiration after wealthy respectability, or who at least were not satisfied with this ideal. Their voices were silenced for the most part during the Prophet's lifetime, after his rôle of world-conqueror had begun, and during the stormy times which preceded the establishment of the Umayyad dynasty they could not easily make themselves heard. The distinction that is sometimes drawn by Islamic writers between the various dynasties as respectively spiritual and temporal, religious and worldly, had no existence in fact; no empire can be anything other than worldly; the pious Caliphs were as anxious about the revenue as were the impious; the practice of assigning annual pensions to the Moslems in order of enrolment was introduced by the second Caliph, and would doubtless have been approved by the Prophet. The Prophet's

---

[1] Ṭabarī ii. 789.   [2] Ibn Khallikan.

cousin, celebrated on the one hand as the "interpreter of the Koran," and on the other as the ancestor of the Abbasid sovereigns, 'Abdallah Ibn 'Abbās, when compelled to quit his governorship of Baṣrah, secured for himself the public treasure. The Prophet's grandson, Ḥasan, son of Ali and Fāṭimah, and one of the personages held in highest reverence by both the chief Islamic sects, sold his claims to the sovereignty for a handsome sum. The unpopularity of the third Caliph, who, however, as the husband of two of the Prophet's daughters, was one of the most highly esteemed among the Moslems, and from an early time was called the possessor of the two lights, was said to be due to his unduly distributing the public treasure among his relations.

The tradition makes the Meccan precursors of Mohammed ascetics, and suggests that many of his followers would have been better pleased had he established a more definitely ascetic system. Doubtless, then, such concessions as he made to this taste were welcome to many of his followers, and certain prohibitions which apply to all Moslems are evidently ascetic in character. The most notable among prohibited enjoyments are those of wine and sport. The sentiment, especially among the humbler Moslems, on these subjects appears to have been regularly in favour of strictness, and though the Umayyad sovereigns are frequently represented by their successors as evil-livers, a fair number among them were against any sort of laxity, while those who were lax thereby rendered their thrones insecure. The fact of a Moslem being given wine in lieu of vinegar by a shopman, who then declined to refund the money, led to a revolt in the year 119.[1] Still, when the world has been found worth winning, it is usually found worth enjoying, and the fortunes amassed by those who took part in the successful wars with Unbelievers were ordinarily consumed in the enjoyment of luxuries of various sorts, though the pleasures particularly forbidden may have often been avoided. The third Caliph, according to the chronicle, confessed his inability to emulate the coarse diet maintained by his two predecessors, even when mounted on the throne. And the first Umayyad Caliph is represented as stating like Solomon that he had enjoyed all that it was possible to enjoy.

A class of persons called variously " ascetics," " devotees," " worshippers," " saintly men," is the subject of occasional allusions in the history of the first two dynasties. In some dying injunctions of the year 82 A.H., " the ethics of the saintly " is recommended as a subject of study.[2] An example of the proper conduct for such persons is given in the chronicle for the year 98 ;[3] a priceless crown has been taken in some plunder, and it occurs to the conqueror to try whether anyone would refuse such a gift. A certain saint is offered it and declines ; it is forced upon his acceptance, and he then presents it to a beggar, from whom the commander reacquires it for a vast sum. Persons of saintly reputation are

---

[1] Ṭabarī ii. 1622.　　　[2] *Ibid.*, 1083.　　　[3] *Ibid.*, 1326.

occasionally employed in minor political rôles; *e.g.*
as messengers to induce subject kings to pay their
tribute;[1] as arbiters in the case of disputes between
commanders;[2] or as preachers dissuading the Moslems from factiousness.[3] At times their studies end
in their rebelling against the powers that be,[4] or
supporting some pretender who will undertake to
live up to their standard. The first use of *wool* in
connection with them appears to be in the year 128,
when one of these fighting ascetics has some of that
material on his standards.[5] Woollen garments, however, not unfrequently figure in narratives of this
period, as the dress of condemned criminals,[6] or of
beggars.[7] The colour white, as the colour of grave-
clothes, is also at this time connected with mourning
and asceticism.[8] By a man's coarse white raiment
it was possible to guess that he was an ascetic,[9]
though he might be either a Moslem ascetic or a
Christian monk; and, indeed, this costume of white
wool is identified sometimes with the attire of monks,
who were supposed by an early Moslem observer to
put it on in order to impress their fellows with the
idea of their saintliness, and so obtain the right to
live in idleness at other people's expense.[10] There

---

[1] Ṭabarī ii. 1228. [2] *Ibid.*, 1386.
[3] *Ibid.*, 1392. [4] *Ibid.*, 1628.
[5] *Ibid.*, 1921. [6] *Ibid.*, 1452.
[7] *Ibid.*, 1351. [8] *Ibid.*, 162; Yāḳūt, Udabā vi. 375.
[9] Mas'ūdī, Murūj ii. 231.

[10] Jāḥiẓ, Ḥayawān i. 103; iv. 137. At a later time the white is
distinguished from the wool as a different degree of mourning.
Ibn Iyās iii. 20.

can be little doubt, then, that the name Ṣūfi means no more than " wearer of wool," and, indeed, a poet who perhaps does not yet know of it as a technical name for ascetic speaks of " time having put on wool," meaning that it has put on mourning.[1]

In the early part of the third century it appears that the Moslem ascetic was not easily distinguished from the Christian ; and, indeed, they had much in common. Their ancestor in the Græco-Roman world was the Cynic, who in the analysis of Epictetus is the Stoic who carries his principles to their logical conclusion, and who, in order that he may be able to defy fortune, gives fortune no pledges. The Cynic in that brilliant description addresses mankind from a higher plane than theirs, for he is free from all their cares and passions. His business requires qualifications no less remarkable and rare than those of the general or the steward.

Where life was lived so much in public, any deviation from ordinary conduct was liable to be suspected and to provoke resentment. In the year 33 a man was summoned to appear before the Caliph on the ground that he was a vegetarian, disapproved of marriage, and failed to attend the Friday service in the mosque.[2] Vegetarianism might seem a harmless enough practice, but it was associated with the name of one Mazdak, who in the century preceding the rise of Islam was supposed to have shaken Persian society to its foundations. In the Wisdom of

---

[1] Abū Tammām ; ridiculed by Mutanabbi, Yāḳūt vi. 514.
[2] Ṭabarī i. 2924

Solomon the "just man" is charged by the others with following a different line of conduct from theirs. And, in fact, it would appear to be the case that ostentatious piety was often the sign of anarchical tendencies and the prelude to revolt. Religion in the first century after the Prophet's death was so closely connected with politics that the earnest Moslem was compelled to take a political line; and that line would be dictated by his attitude towards those who had started and taken part in the civil wars. The greatest devotees appear to have regularly been against both the Umayyads and the party which recognised the right of the Prophet's family to succeed; their devotion was accompanied by a ruthlessness which shocked their less religious contemporaries. Still, it is clear that there were pious men who kept out of the world altogether, and were in favour of nothing but peace and order, so far as they occupied themselves with the affairs of their time at all. The "conduct of the pious," which, as we have seen, developed into a subject of study by the year 82, was then elaborated by these persons, who in the main exaggerated or amplified what they found recommended in the Koran.

For the Umayyad period we possess few documents which testify to these persons' activity, but in the Abbasid period the ascetic becomes an institution. In part he attracts attention by his attitude towards the world, wherein he is without being of it; the prizes for which others contend have no attraction for him. But he is also the preacher whose words have the power to produce ecstasy, or at least elevate the hearer.

Of the first of these preachers who also figured as an author we possess several works in MS. They seem to follow the lines of the Christian sermon, to the extent even of reproducing matter from the New Testament; they are fervent, and their moral tone is high; yet it is difficult to imagine their producing that ecstasy among their audience with which they are credited. They seem quite free from the elaborate technicalities with which the later Ṣūfi treatises abound.

A certain amount of licence is ordinarily allowed the preacher in his treatment of history, for his lessons must be enforced by references to patterns of conduct, whence the tendency arises to accommodate history to his ideals. As one of the later Ṣūfis expresses it, the authority of a great name is wanted for something, and no harm seems to be done if a man is credited with some extra virtues.

The use in these homiletic works of matter taken directly from Christian sources is sufficiently remarkable to justify us in finding Christian influence or the survival of Christian ideals at the base of the movement. Sometimes the matter is taken over bodily; thus the Parable of the Sower is told by the earliest Ṣūfi writer. Abū Ṭālib takes over the dialogue in the Gospel eschatology between the Saviour and those who are taunted with having seen Him hungry and refused Him food; only for the questioner he substitutes Allah, and for " the least of these " his Moslem brother. Not a few of the Beatitudes are taken over, sometimes with the name of their author. Commonplaces which are found in Christian homiletic works reappear with little or no alteration in the Ṣūfi sermons. In the Acts of Thomas, the Apostle, when employed by a king to build a palace, spends the money in charity to the poor. Presently the king's brother dies, and finds that a wonderful palace has been built for the king in Paradise with the alms which Thomas bestowed in his name. This story reappears in the doctrine of Abū Ṭālib that when a poor man takes charity from the wealthy, he is thereby building him a house in Paradise.[1]

One name which Ṣūfism takes over from Christian theorists is *gnosis*. As early as the Epistles of St Paul we read of a "wisdom" or esoteric doctrine which is only communicated to those that are advanced spiritually; and we know that in later times at any rate that gnosis was something very different from ordinary orthodoxy. This same word "knowledge" is also employed by the Ṣūfis as a technical description of their system, and indeed as the substitute which God has given them for the world.[2] In the later developments "knowledge" branches out into three forms, which we might render "knowledge," "acquaintance," and "understanding." The third is the highest stage, and the person who attains to it is all but deified.

Here, however, as in the case of jurisprudence, the

---

[1] Ḳ. Ḳ, ii. 201.   [2] *Ibid.*, ii. 193.

amount taken over from earlier communities does not appear to have been considerable. It would seem fairly clear that the ascetic is an early institution in the East; and even in the West there is a lurking feeling of respect for the man who is above caring for what constitute the object of ordinary aspirations. When once men begin to speculate upon this instinct, the system necessarily goes through a number of stages — not unlike the stages which the ascetics claim to go through individually. It is difficult to maintain that present fortune may be prudently resigned for a future of the same kind; hence the ascetic quickly becomes dissatisfied with a sensual Paradise. The search after a substitute for that Paradise leads on to the next stage, the doctrine of the love of God and *nirvana*. Probably ideas originally taken from Plato had somehow found their way into these men's minds, just as Aristotelianism is traceable in the Koran; but the influence is very indirect and has come tortuously.

That volume not unjustly calls attention to its miscellaneous character, and though it by no means despises the acquisition of spoil in this world, and condemns lavish expenditure, whilst promising the faithful in Paradise delights greater in quantity but not differing in quality from what they might enjoy down here, still it occasionally takes a line more in accordance with ascetic spiritualism; it pronounces the favour of God to be a better thing than talents of gold and the like. Moreover, the theory of atonement at any rate gives some hints as to the sort of acts which win God's favour; if offences can be atoned by charity or fasting, it is clear that these acts must possess positive value; otherwise they could not serve as makeweights against such negative quantities as sins. And there is a tendency to extend the theory of atonement to all religious observances; since God does nothing in vain, the purpose of these performances must be to atone for acts committed wittingly or unwittingly which have incurred God's displeasure. The first line wherein asceticism can develop is, then, that of supererogation: doing what the Koran prescribes to a more liberal extent than it actually enjoins. And so far as Islamic asceticism is expressed in practice, it regularly adopts this method. It wins merit by excessive performance of those acts which on the authority of the Koran are known to win it.

The work from which the details to be given in this lecture are mainly taken is of the fourth century of Islam, by which time asceticism had long been recognised as an institution with many provincial varieties. Possibly the earliest place with which it is connected is Kufah, the city which showed so infelicitous a devotion to the Prophet's family. The "conduct of the saints," which, as has been seen, had become a recognised subject of study before the end of the first century, had by the fourth acquired considerable proportions; fairly copious hagiologies had by that time been amassed, and numerous sayings of an edifying nature either recorded of or attributed to the saints. The question of the accuracy of these legends is of little importance ; what they indicate is the general notion of sanctity current, and what view of life a saint was expected to take. Although, then, we have ordinarily restricted ourselves to authorities who are not later than the third century, in this particular matter we are not likely to be led into serious error by employing a work of the fourth. As earlier sources of information become open to us, we constantly find the doctrines and the statements which are to be found in the later works anticipated ; even the astounding perversions of the Koran which are usually associated with the mysticism of the sixth century are to be found with little divergence in the mysticism of the third. The mystics are not only like the jurists conservative, but show a tendency to preserve theories and practices which are immemorial, and which have accidentally adopted Islam as their local attire.

The five daily *ṣalawāt* might be thought to constitute a considerable devotional exercise, since each of them occupies some minutes. How they came to assume their stereotyped form will never be known ; it is clear that their purpose is rather "making mention of God," and keeping the mind in constant recollection of the Divine Being, than petition or supplication. To the devout these five daily exercises did not nearly suffice ; their aim was rather to occupy the whole day and night with devotion of the kind, and numerous different rites were devised compassing this end. Traditions were invented promising greater and ever greater rewards to those

who practised these extra devotions; their spurious-
ness was evident, and probably little importance was
attached to them.

The extra devotions invented by the ascetics and
mystics introduced into Islam something far more
analogous to the prayers of other religions than the
ṣalāt. Abū Ṭālib al-Mekkī prescribes forms for use
on lying down and rising which do not differ materially
from the prayers recommended in Christian manuals
of devotion; what is solicited is preservation from
the dangers of the day and of the night. But with
the limitation of human desires which the ascetic
system compasses, the number of possible requests is
naturally reduced. The discipline which frees the
mind from worldly desire very soon liberates it from
all desires for the next world also: the prospect of
Hell-fire itself, from which religion at the start
promises immunity, comes to be contemplated with
indifference; hence even these prayers tend to
become confessions rather than supplications, and
the blessings which they procure become immaterial
—immunity from forgetting the text of the Koran or
sleeping when the saint should be vigilant.

In the matter of the *ṣalāt* or regular devotion enjoined by the code, the Ṣūfis endeavour to spiritualise
the ceremony by making it an occasion for complete
abstraction from the world. Some saints could boast
that for forty years they had said their devotions
without knowing who was on their right side or on
their left. *Ṣalāt* was rendered void if the mind of
the devotee admitted any thought besides: if, *e.g.*,

he read anything written on wall or carpet. The formulæ should not be pronounced as such, but out of conviction: when a man says "Allah is greater," he should, tacitly indeed, but because he is convinced of its truth, add "than the great." But in order to say this he must in his own mind subordinate all else to God; for otherwise he will be saying what he does not mean. There were saints who when they started their *ṣalāt* told their women-folk that they might chatter as much as they liked and even beat drums: they were too much absorbed in prayer to hear, however loud the noise. When one of them was saying his *ṣalāt* in the mosque of Baṣrah a column fell, bringing down with it an erection of four storeys; he continued praying, and when after he had finished the people congratulated him on his escape, he asked what from. Great names were quoted for the practice of praying hastily, and so shortening the time taken by the devotion as to give Satan no chance of distracting the thoughts.

The Islamic Fast is an obscure subject, as it seems to belong in origin to some system with which we are unfamiliar, although it contains Jewish and Christian elements also. With the Christians, fasting seems regularly to have meant not complete abstinence, but abstinence from dainties; and, indeed, unless fasting is to interfere seriously with the business of life, this would seem to be the best interpretation of the process; food is retained as a necessity, but the element of enjoyment is so far as possible abstracted. The Jewish theory is that fasting means complete abstinence from food, but then they fast for one complete day only: which is not sufficient to permanently injure the health. The Mohammedan theory of fasting is complete abstinence, but only during the day: the substitution of the night for the day as the feeding time, for a period somewhat shorter than the Christian forty days, yet during a month which from its name must at one time have been part of the hot summer. This institution clearly was useful as military discipline, seeing that the night was the best time for forays; yet it is not quite easy to think of it as a substitute for the Jewish fasts, although the text of the Koran expressly asserts that this is so. What the Koranic ordinance has in common with those of the older systems is the prescription of a number of days for this purpose; but the reason assigned for the choice of Ramaḍān is that in that month the Koran was revealed—it must be supposed was revealed for the first time. The connection of ideas seems to be this: it appears from Deuteronomy ix. 9 that Moses fasted on the mountain forty days and forty nights, and at the end of the time received the Law. With this fast of Moses the Christian fast of forty days is not unnaturally confused; the latter is supposed to be commemorative of the former. From the text of Surah ii., then, we learn that the Moslem fast is similarly commemorative of the descent of the Koran, which the tradition connects with a similar period of asceticism; this the Koran does not assert, though it perhaps implies it; and in Surah vii. 138 we see how the number forty is reduced to a month. The original appointment with Moses was for thirty days; these "we supplemented with ten, so that the appointment with his Lord was made up to forty days." The forty days, then, represented an increase on an original thirty, or one whole month. And to this month the Koranic legislation returns. How the particular mode of fasting originated it might be hard to conjecture.

Fasting was regarded by the Ṣūfis not only as a devotional exercise, but as a pious act pleasing to God, whence on the one hand it is assigned propitiatory value in the Koran itself, whilst on the other the devout were by no means satisfied with a fast of thirty days in the whole year; they endeavour to extend the limits. Monday and Thursday in each week are prescribed as fast days, wherein perhaps we see the principle of antedating the Christian fasts, somewhat as the Friday anticipates the Sabbath and the Sunday. Calculations came to be made of the amount of the year which it was desirable to fast, and some care had to be exercised to see that the special glories of Ramaḍān were not obscured, as would be the case if similar sanctity attached to the whole year. Fasting every other day, fasting two days out of three, fasting one day out of three, were all commended practices. Nevertheless, the doctrine is sometimes heard that the true fasting is abstinence from the gratification of evil passions, and that the fasting of the heart is a more important matter than the fasting of the frame.

It seems clear that fasting in the Ṣūfi sense means something different from the normal fasting of Ramaḍān, and has nothing to do with the substitution of night for day as the meal-time. It means abstinence from food of all sorts. Help towards fasting was got from the Ṣūfi melodies; when these were sung they reminded the devotee of his spiritual needs and caused him to forget the pangs of hunger.

But besides this, some methods could be suggested whereby the aspirant could accustom himself to the minimum of nourishment necessary to keep body and soul together. This could be done either by reducing the amount to one-third of what was usual, or by increasing the number of hours to elapse between meals. One meal in seventy-two hours was thought to be in ordinary cases the attainable limit. The test whether food was taken to gratify the appetite or merely to allay the pangs of hunger might be either the desire for bread without relish of any sort, or inability to distinguish between bread and other foods; one who desired a particular food, and not food generically, was not really hungry.[1] A somewhat less savoury test was to see whether a fly settled on the saliva; if none did, the aspirant might be satisfied that he was really hungry.

Cases of longer abstinence than that suggested were narrated among the glories of various saints. Fasts of five or six days were not uncommon; a vision of power from the spiritual world would appear to one who fasted forty days; a Ṣūfi converted

---

[1] Ḳ. Ḳ. ii. 165.

a Christian monk by showing that he could fast sixty days successively, and so beat the Biblical records.

Naturally the theory of fasting was extended to vetoing all refinements in diet; the coarser the food and the simpler, the better it corresponded with the Ṣūfi ideal. Some disapproved of the chase and food so acquired because of the cruelty inflicted on the animals.[1] The change of raiment which the asceticism of the gospel condemned was also tabooed by the Ṣūfis. The hungering and thirsting after righteousness in the evangelical beatitude was interpreted of actual hunger and thirst; and similarly, the Prophet is credited with the saying, " Whoso among you is most filled in this life shall fast longest on the Day of Judgment." Satan is said to follow the course of the blood in the human body; the contraction of the veins which was said to be produced by fasting would render it harder for him to get about.

To a certain extent the Ṣūfic fasting and simplicity of diet was based on medical theory, and the Prophet's supposed prescription of one-third the usual amount is said to have won warm eulogies from the faculty. It could be shown that the temperature of the stomach, *i.e.*, as Aristotle had taught, the proportion between hot and cold, dry and moist, was least disturbed by water, wheaten bread, partridge meat, and pomegranate or citron. And, indeed, according to Moslem authorities the cosmogony of the Old Testament contained not only the four Aristotelian elements, but the doctrine of the four humours of the body besides.[2]

---

[1] Ḥayawān iv. 137.   [2] Ḳ. Ḳ. ii. 170.

The Aristotelian philosophy could be employed in defence of the fasting-doctrine in another way. Wahb Ibn Munabbih, who is responsible for the last quotation from the Torah, observed that the stomach was the mean in the body; and the secret of doing right lay in getting hold of the mean. He, therefore, who had his stomach in full control was also in control of his other members. But if the stomach was allowed to get the upper hand, the result was a general mutiny among them.

Edifying stories connected with fasting are collected by Abū Ṭālib, some of which have their interest. A Ṣūfi desired rice-bread and fish for twenty years, but each time he felt the desire he resisted it. After death he appeared to a friend in a dream. The delights of Paradise were ineffable, he said; immediately on his arrival he had been served with rice-bread and fish. The Prophet appeared in a dream to a man who had fasted thirty years; not even eating bread. The Prophet seized his arm, and exclaimed: Hast thou fasted thus? As he did not tell the ascetic to stop fasting, the latter continued his mode of life. 'Utbah asked 'Abd al-Wāhid Ibn Zaid why a fellow-devotee had attained a stage of spiritual elevation higher than his own: he was told that it was by not eating dates. If he too left off eating them, he would attain to the same level. 'Utbah shed tears when told of this; which the teacher excused on the ground that if 'Utbah once resolved to break with a habit, he could be counted upon never to resume it.

Granting that food must at certain times be taken—
and there were ascetics who even feasted on certain
occasions—the number of points to be observed in
connection therewith is no fewer than one hundred
and seventy ;[1] whence it may be doubted whether
Islam is, after all, so simple as has been thought.
Many of these points would seem to belong to
elementary etiquette, or at best to fashion; yet the
pious Umayyad Omar II. thought some of them
sufficiently important to be regulated by rescripts.

To the employment of hunger as a means of grace
must be added the employment of illness. Even in
Plato, who as a Greek favoured the development of
physical strength and beauty, we find the suggestion
that men are at times led to become philosophers
by illness; and since the holy war cannot well be
carried on except by men in full physical vigour, we
fancy the Prophet would have absolutely rejected the
doctrine that ill-health should be cultivated. The
Ṣūfis, however, who thought only of spiritual warfare,
naturally perceived that Satan, in the sense of the
lusts of the eye and flesh and the pride of life, could be
defeated with greater ease by the sickly than by the
strong. What tempted Pharaoh to claim divinity
was the fact that he had lived four hundred years
without suffering fever or headache. Further, sick-
ness has propitiatory value : a day's fever atones
for a year's misdeeds. Health, then, to the Ṣūfis
signifies mental or spiritual health ; a man is in good
health when he is free from transgression. The loss

<hr>

[1] Ḳ. Ḳ. ii. 179.

of any member or faculty took away the possibility of transgressing; whence some of the Companions of the Prophet were credited with desiring to be blind. Although the Prophet was an authority on medicine as on other subjects, the morality of employing curatives was questioned; for there was the danger that the effect apparently produced by the drug might be ascribed to the drug, and the patient or physician become in his secret thoughts a polytheist —recognising some power other than God in the world. On the other hand, it was clear that the postures to be adopted in the daily devotion required that the body should be in a condition of vigour: one saint, therefore, who was paralysed obtained by prayer the use of his limbs for those daily devotions: so soon as they were over he became bedridden as before.

Still deeper meanings were found in illness. Sahl refused to treat himself for a malady which he cured in others, because a blow from the beloved did not pain. The saint's consciousness of God was clearest when he was in fever.

Just as speculation on the meaning and purpose of fasting led to "perpetual fasting," for if fasting were a virtuous act, there was no reason why it should be reserved for a particular time of the year, so speculation led to some modification of the doctrine of the pilgrimage. In the case of this institution we have a difficulty similar to that of which the Pentateuch gives evidence: where a feast is held within or in the immediate neighbourhood of a city or village, it is possible for the whole community to join in the celebration; for an occasional holiday interferes with the work of no one, and even the suspension of all business for a short period is possible. But where the feasting-place is at a distance, various difficulties come in; since few occupations can be neglected for many days at a time, and the quitting of habitations for months together by the whole population would be ruinous; a yearly pilgrimage might be contemplated by a nomad tribe, but would be impossible in the case of one that was settled. The text of the Koran therefore enjoins the pilgrimage on all who can take part in it;[1] but whereas it apparently prescribes pilgrimage not once in a lifetime, but every year, it also leaves it open to the Moslem to make his pilgrimage in one or other of several months, and leaves it to him to fix the time. It merely enjoins on him the performance of certain ceremonies and abstinence from certain acts during the time in which he chooses to perform the rite. The old employment of the pilgrimage as a fair or meeting for the exchange of merchandise is permitted, so far as it does not interfere with these prescriptions.

The Koranic texts are obscure, and the interpreters are evidently embarrassed by them; this, however, appears to be the natural sense. The extension of the Islamic empire to distances which even the Prophet can scarcely have contemplated rendered the annual performance of the rite impossible for

---

[1] iii. 91.

many members of the community, and exceedingly irksome to others; hence the theory that it should be performed once at least in a lifetime. Moreover, the days when certain special ceremonies were usual apparently came to be thought of as the most important part of the feast; hence the wide limits permitted in the Koran were restricted, and a distinction was made between the minor pilgrimage, of which the time was fixed by the devotee, and the major pilgrimage, of which the time was fixed by the law. And though annual pilgrimage was regarded as meritorious, the name "pilgrimage of Islam" was given to that which a Believer performed once in his lifetime, any other being supererogatory.

But the question arose: if residence in Meccah were meritorious, if it meant in reality neighbourhood to God, how came it that one visit of a few days was sufficient? Ought not the devotee to reside there all his life? Hence there were persons who followed this argument to its logical conclusion, and earned the title "neighbour of Allah." But others felt more inclined to spiritualise the precept, and make the pilgrimage allegorical; the intellectual journey was to serve instead of the actual. A man who had provided 2000 dirhems for journey money to Meccah was told by a saint that he could acquire more merit by disbursing them in charity than by going on pilgrimage with them;[1] the very thought of preferring the pilgrimage to the charity was a sign that the man's soul had been blinded by greed.

[1] Ḳ. Ḳ. i. 95.

To the ceremonies of the pilgrimage there was no occasion to make any addition; that institution already contained a number which originally had belonged to different sanctuaries and different cults. One point wherein the ordinary interpretation of the precept could be straitened was with regard to the period of life wherein it should be undertaken; and Abū Ṭālib decides that a man should make the pilgrimage so soon as the act is within his power. From the words of the Prophet at the Farewell Pilgrimage it was inferred that no man was a complete Moslem who had not yet gone through this ceremony; Omar, it was said, had thought of imposing the poll-tax on all who had not yet performed it, since they were no better than Jews or Christians. Some authorities held that no prayers should be said over the graves of wealthy Moslems who had failed to carry out this obligation, and texts of the Koran wherein the lost solicit a return to this world in order to make good omissions were interpreted of this ceremony.

Then some additional merit could be acquired by rendering the journey, which in any case was fatiguing, additionally difficult. Any invention or appliance which was calculated to increase the rider's comfort was to be condemned; the same was to be held of all ostentation or display of wealth; the colour red in particular was to be avoided. The employment of luxurious litters on this occasion was said to have been an innovation of the notorious Ḥajjāj Ibn Yūsuf, an Umayyad governor whose name became proverbial for tyranny and ruthlessness, and who might with certainty be reckoned among the lost.[1] The most meritorious procedure was to walk; but, since the course which caused the greatest amount of discomfort was the best, probably the sound reply was that of a jurist who held that the person to whom the hiring of a mount occasioned more mental anguish than walking, had better hire.

In the matter of sacrifice the oldest system of valuation was retained: the more valuable the animal the better the sacrifice: quality was to be considered above quantity. Omar was offered the price of thirty beasts for the beast which he proposed to sacrifice, but was told by the Prophet to refuse. The list of possible blemishes in the animal to be offered is made out with an elaboration which we miss even in the Levitical code. It may be observed that the Koran is no less positive than the Hebrew Prophets that God can have no possible use for a slaughtered animal; but this hardihood in theory was not accompanied by similar hardihood in practice; it was not for the Prophet of Allah to deprive Allah of any honour which had previously been paid him.

Further, it was possible to divest the feast of all festive elements by emphasising the seriousness of the occasion; the same transformation was to be effected as that which the teaching of St Paul brought about in the Christian love-feasts. So far as possible the pilgrim was to fast and maintain silence; his service might count on acceptance if he made his pilgrimage

---

[1] Jāḥiz, Ḥayawān iv. 146.

an occasion to substitute pious for impious associates, and meditation on serious matters for sport. In Meccah only were men responsible for evil thoughts and punishable for entertaining them. Omar said he would rather commit seventy sins elsewhere than one in Meccah ; and there were pilgrims who pitched two tents, one within and one outside the sacred area, in order to be safe. And the danger which resulted from the extreme sanctity of Meccah was probably the reason why the " neighbourhood of Allah " was not ordinarily thought desirable. Besides this, it was clear that familiarity could not fail to produce a certain amount of contempt, or at least diminution of reverence ; Meccah at a distance was more glorious than it appeared to a resident. To this consideration there was to be added the sordid and mundane one that everything was costly at Meccah, although, according to some, it was sinful to take rent for houses or apartments in the sacred city.

The Ṣūfi precepts on the subject of almsgiving agree almost verbally with those of the Sermon on the Mount, and doubtless to some extent are traceable to that source. " Let not thy left hand know what thy right hand doeth " is the form adopted for the regulation of the procedure ; the expression is defended as the sort of exaggeration tolerated by the Arabic language, and parallels to it are cited from the Koran. As in the Sermon on the Mount, any ostentation in charity is said to annul the merit thereby acquired, and some ingenious modes are recorded whereby the givers of charity endeavoured to conceal their personalities. Where such concealment is not practised, still the attitude of the giver should be humble, the recipient so far as possible spared all humiliation; since it is the giver who is according to the etymological theory of charity purified by the gift, he should acknowledge that the recipient is his superior; and though it is the duty of the recipient to render thanks, it is his duty towards God, and is not a claim which the giver should try to enforce. For it is the reward of God which the giver should seek to obtain, and he cannot expect a double reward for the same act. The gift, it is said, goes into the hand of God before it goes into the hand of the recipient; and those recipients are to be preferred who thank God only for the gift. This is the moral of the story of 'Ā'ishah, who when there came the revelation defending her honour, declared that God was to be thanked for it, not Mohammed — who, it appears, had harboured doubts concerning her innocence.

Since the giving of alms is a matter wherein two participate, there is necessarily some little conflict of interests, giving rise to differences of opinion. It would seem to be the interest of the giver that the gift should be kept secret, since only thus can its sincerity be assured; on the other hand, it is the interest of the recipient that it should be public, since the latter ought to harbour no false pride. Again, it is to the spiritual interest of the giver that the gift should be as large as possible, whereas the recipient should take the least which necessity permits. The

saint Junaid—perhaps before the days of his conversion—hearing that another saint held out his
hand for gifts with the view of enabling wealthy
people to obtain merit in the next world, sent
a hundred dirhems plus some unknown quantity.
The recipient accepted the unknown quantity, but
returned the hundred dirhems; since God would
accept only that which was sent on the principle
that the right hand should not know what the left
hand doeth. Others refused gifts offered in public
and accepted them in private, alleging that it was
unlawful to give alms in public and they could not
countenance breaches of the law, or more naïvely
confessing that they disliked the humiliation. Yet
another theory, which neglected the intermediaries
and saw no cause but God, ignored the difference
between the hidden and the open, and made no
distinction between the public and the private alms.
Abū Ṭālib makes the whole question one of casuistry,
to be settled by the character of individual donors
and recipients, the general principle being that the
giver should conceal and the taker reveal.

The apparent simplicity of the Koranic teaching
was thus gradually altered into elaborate ritualism;
and the moderation of Islam was forgotten. The
weekly day of worship, which was almost a surrogate
for the Saturday and Sunday of the Jews and
Christians, since the text of the Koran expressly
permits the conduct of business except actually
during the time when public worship is going on,
became assimilated to those other days of rest,

although it seems clear that the Prophet regarded the Jewish Sabbath as anything but a blessing to the community which observed it. The permission to transact business was interpreted away as permission to ask God's favour by prayer. Special merit was assigned to an early appearance in the mosque; he was to be accounted a lukewarm Moslem who only arrived in time to take part in the midday worship. Men were enjoined to put on festal attire; a tradition ascribed to the Prophet made the Friday bath obligatory. Both sexes should employ perfume: the men such as displayed its odour but concealed its colour; the women such as concealed its odour but displayed its colour. The visit to the mosque on the Friday was to be thought of as a visit to the House of God, wherein the ceremonies usual when the humble visit the great should be observed. The turban should not be removed from the head, at any rate while the public service is going on; for that curious difference between Eastern and Western etiquette is emphasised here also. Otherwise the Friday is to be regarded as a day of rest, yet in the Puritan sense: pleasure is as reprehensible therein as work. The term work is not, of course, applied to religious study; but any other sort should be avoided. Even the collection which forms part of most Christian services finds some imitation. The giving of alms at the conclusion of the Friday service is specially meritorious.

The transference of a feast into a fast is noteworthy, but belongs to a whole class of phenomena depending

on the spiritualisation of religion, whereas our word
" holiday " illustrates either the reverse process, or the
persistence in stereotyped form of the earlier notion
attaching to holiness.   Fasting on the Friday is
recommended by some saints—whether in imitation
of Christians or because holiness is associated with
fasting rather than with feasting. The laying in a
stock of provisions on the Thursday for use on the
Friday is deprecated : only spiritual provisions should
be laid in.

The fancy of pious Moslems was largely occupied
with devising myths on the subject of the Friday ;
besides being the day whereon Adam was created, it
was also the day of his fall and the day of his death ;
the two last scarcely reasons for festive commemora-
tion. Like the Christian Sunday it is also to be the
day of the Resurrection. Just as the Jewish Sabbath
is thought to be kept by the Deity Himself, so there
is a tradition that every Friday Allah performs a
great act of manumission, which with mankind is
especially pious : He releases sixty thousand souls that
are imprisoned in Hell.

Special forms of prayer were invented for the
Friday by the Prophet Idrīs, and the saint Ibrāhīm
Ibn Adham : their employment ensures the vouch-
safing of whatever the Believer requests ; but, indeed,
there is some particular time on the Friday when
prayer is quite certain to be answered. There are,
however, great differences of opinion as to the loca-
tion of this moment, and some deny that it can be
located. It is comparable to the Night of Kadar,

which is some night but no particular night in Ramaḍān.

Up to this point we have only traced the channels through which the Islamic ascetics worked their way to higher things, or at least to notions whose abstractness contrasts singularly with the materialism of the Koran, and the political and military rôle which the Islamic Prophet played. Their exercises and speculations, as will be seen, led them still further from the doctrines of the Koran, and exposed them to the censure and even execration of orthodox jurists who might have been prepared to accompany them in their earlier stages. So long, however, as their procedure was confined to exaggerated observance of Koranic institutions they won the respect of their fellows, and earned the right to rebuke vice, and in general to look after the morals of the community. And even when their extravagances brought upon them official censure, and even terrible punishments, their memory was apt to be cherished by the masses, whom their saintliness had impressed.

LECTURE VI

IF we have hitherto found the ascetic occupied
with exaggeration of the four performances enjoined
by Islam, we shall now find him developing unlooked-
for consequences from the primary proposition of the
system—there is no God but Allah, with Whom
nothing must be associated. The sense of the former
expression naturally depends on the meaning to be
assigned to the word "god," whereon the pious
perhaps preferred not to speculate; but the meaning
of "association" could be studied without danger,
and it followed that nothing else might be admitted
into any sphere where God was to be found. If, *e.g.*,
God is to be loved, then nothing else may be loved;
any other object of affection would be associated with
God, and the person who bestowed the affection
would be a pagan. The same argument excludes all
desires; if the worshipper's object is Paradise, then
he is desiring something besides God, and so is a
polytheist. The notion thereby comes in that the
ceremonies enjoined by the code have only disciplinary value, as helps to the attainment of the
true knowledge and realisation of the divine unity.

Whence we shall find that the most advanced among the mystics declared that these performances were no longer necessary in their case, but were to be kept up, if at all, for the edification of the vulgar. They formed part of a discipline to be undergone in pursuit of an end.

Most of the ascetic practices enumerated could be summed up in the word "poverty," since that at which the Ṣūfi aims is to undergo out of choice the privations which the poor man undergoes out of necessity. Doubtless the chief merit lies in the privation being voluntary; and in general there is a tendency in all hagiologies to demonstrate that the saints were in origin persons of wealth and station who had voluntarily abandoned what most men prize. But if the enjoyment of luxuries is absolutely wicked, it would seem clear that poverty has the advantage of safety. And this premise is certainly assumed. Severe as are the doctrines formulated by Abū Ṭālib on the subject of hospitality, he mentions five reasons which justify a man who has accepted an invitation to a meal in going away leaving it untasted; one is the employment by the host of silver plate, to the extent even of the stopper of a vessel. Aḥmad Ibn Ḥanbal before the Inquisition was invited to a banquet, and accepted the invitation; seeing a silver vessel on the cloth he rose and left, his disciples or admirers following him; as may be imagined, to the consternation of the host, who had reason to be thankful that they had not followed their convictions to the extent of damaging the goods. Similarly, the

presence of satin is a justification for quitting ; anyone who by staying assents to the employment of
such a luxury becomes a participator in the crime.

Hence we get a series of aphorisms attributed to
the Prophet containing glowing eulogies of poverty,
though we should have thought the Prophet had had
far too great experience of affairs to take such a view
seriously. Similar aphorisms are ascribed to leading
saints ; piety amid wealth is like a garden growing
on a dunghill ; where there is poverty it is like a pearl
necklace on a fair woman.

The notion of poverty is, of course, a relative one,
and since wealth means storage of provisions, the
completest poverty is where there is no store of any
sort, and the poor man is also a beggar. This mode
of life does not appear to have had the Prophet's
approval, and he is even said, in accepting the submission or conversion of some tribes, to have stipulated
that they should not beg. The limit of storage is
fixed by the Koranic statement that God made an
appointment with Moses for the fortieth day ; for
if a man may count on living forty days, it follows
that he has a licence to store for forty days. The
better theory is doubtless that death should be
expected momentarily, whence only a minimum of
storage should be permitted. A mendicant Ṣūfī to
whom a purse containing hundreds of dirhems was
given, had spent the whole by supper-time and had to
beg for that meal. He explained that he had not
expected to live so long ; had he done so, he would
have saved up for it.

To some extent the admiration and cultivation of poverty is limited by the fatalistic doctrine according to which a man's *rizk* or fortune is settled by God, whence he can no more evade it than he can escape death ; he who rejects a windfall is rejecting a gift of God, and so is committing an act of ingratitude and discourtesy. There would appear to be considerable variety not only in fortunes, but in the places in which fortune, or at any rate sustenance, is assigned ; some persons will find it in ten thousand places, others only in one. A saint who left the city to live in the desert in the belief that God would send him his provision there, after a week was near dying of starvation : when he returned to the town he found supplies flowing in from all sides.

Humility, or rather humiliation, is to be practised by the aspirant to unheard-of degrees. A man complained to Bistāmī that in spite of constant fasting and prayer he could not attain to the experiences of the saints. Bistāmī told him that the reason of this was that he still harboured some pride ; the exercise that he recommended was that the man should take a bag of nuts, collect the street arabs round him, and offer a nut to any boy who cuffed him ; the aspirant refused the suggestion, and Bistāmī declined to offer another. A Ṣūfi stole the best clothes from a public bath, and exhibited his booty for no other purpose than that he might become the object of public contempt and reprobation. Some begged that alms might be put into their hands, only because with the Arabs it was thought humiliating to have anything put into the palm. The process which the ascetic should go through is not unlike that which Plato recommends the just man; he should find no fault when charged with capital offences; he should chafe under no depreciation or detraction. He should feel no pleasure when he is praised. Christ is said to have pointed out that things grow in the mould, and the divine knowledge only takes root in a heart that is like the mould in abasement. Humility is their trade like the sweeper's or the scavenger's. Yet this humility is external only: and it is even defined as being too proud to be proud. The Ṣūfi who willingly casts his lot with the lowest is prepared to say Glory to me! in his identification of himself with the object of his adoration. He can take liberties with God which to ordinary men seem blasphemous.

Just as the Ṣūfi should be satisfied with ill-health, so he should practise resignation in things great and small. He should not complain of the weather; he should not say poverty is a trial and a family a nuisance; he should say, like Ibn Mas'ūd, " Wealth and poverty are a pair of steeds, I care not which of the two I ride."

According to this doctrine he has no more right to find 'fault with prosperity than with adversity; finding fault at all is ingratitude, which in the Arabic idiom is synonymous with unbelief. Anas, who served the Prophet ten years, never heard him find fault with anything, or complain of omission or com- mission. When an ancient prophet prayed to be delivered from poverty, he was shown that this prayer meant a rewriting of the whole system of events foreordained by God: by repeating this prayer he would forfeit his claim to be written in the book of life.

Examples are quoted of the degree of resignation which some of the saints aspired to attain. One who claimed to be little more than a beginner expressed his willingness to be damned alone among mankind. Another who acknowledged to having got on a little way was satisfied to be the bridge over Hell whereby the saved will pass, and when all mankind had passed over him, to fill Hell by himself, in order that the oath of God, who had sworn to fill it, might not be violated. A saint who had been bedridden with dropsy thirty years repudiated sympathy, because he liked best what God liked best. One whose prayers were by the Prophet's blessing always answered, and so healed numbers who solicited his aid, was asked why he did not pray that he might recover his own sight: he replied that God's will was to him a better thing.

Since resignation cannot easily be displayed save where there are troubles, the theory that misfortunes are a just cause for glorification speedily arises. No one of you, said a preacher, will meet God without having lied to Him: meaning without having concealed some misfortune: if one had a golden finger, he would parade it; if he had a broken finger, he would conceal it.

A question which suggested itself was the attitude which the devotee should adopt towards death:

should he desire it for the sake of meeting God ; or should he prefer to live because life was all trouble and service ; or should he not mind—have no wish either way ? Clearly the last had attained the ideal state and was above the other two ; but the relative merits of the other two might be the subject of discussion. There was always the danger in the case of the lover of life that he might be mistaken about his real motive : he might confuse what was in reality a physical repulsion to death with the desire to exhibit resignation ; the true attitude towards life and death was that of the water in a well : it remained there without choice of its own, ready at any time to be drawn.

This attitude of complete passivity seems something very different from the active life of the followers of the Prophet, with its fierce enmities and warm loves. The only way wherein the two theories of life could be reconciled was by the doctrine that the devotee should be in complete sympathy with God, and share His loves and hates.

Hence we come back to personal choice, and the doctrine of resignation is not found to work. The mystic Sirrī Sakatī gave up his business because he had said " Thank God " when he was told that all the shops in the street had been burned down except his ; he uttered this exclamation, but immediately became conscious of its selfishness, and selling all he had, gave it to the poor. Discontent, then, was what first started him on the road to resignation.

Probably the conduct of Sirrī Sakatī will be found

philanthropic and commendable ; but we fancy that the Ṣūfī is unable to maintain his transmutation of values very long ; they have an extraordinary tendency to come back, and be assumed as current after they have definitely been repudiated. If loss of property is not a fit subject for complaint, it is not clear why this saint should have adopted this course ; his thanking God was not an act that required thirty years' atonement. And the willingness which these saints display to endure Hell-fire seriously invalidates the threats of the Koran ; for only that can be used as an effective threat which men will avoid to the very uttermost.

Difficulties and contradictions also arise from the maxim of sympathising with God's loves and hates. To the Prophet this maxim was simple enough : God loved those who acknowledged His Prophet, hated those who rejected him. But in the more complicated conditions of the later Islamic states this simple distinction was insufficient : the whole population by no means consisted of saints. Hence high authority was quoted for the doctrine that a man who was beloved by his neighbours was necessarily a hypocrite.

The cultivation of poverty, humiliation, and resignation belong to the negative aspect of the first proposition of the creed ; if the word "god" signifies an object of attachment, then the ascetic who follows the discipline which has been sketched has clearly severed bonds which ordinarily attach men to other things than God ; but there is also the positive side of the proposition to be considered—and this is summed up in the phrase "love of God." That notion is, of course, taken over from older systems, and is found in the Koran. The erotic sentiment, which is rarely quite absent from religion, has probably been identified with it by the Ṣūfis more than by any other devotees. Wives are supposed to have left their husbands because the love of God tolerated no other affection besides itself. The woman saint Rabī'ah 'Adwiyyah rejected one proposal of marriage after another, declining the most munificent offers, on the ground that the whole of the suitors' fortune was not good enough to distract her mind from the thought of God for a single instant. Some wonderful verses wherein she described her sentiment are preserved :

> " I love thee with two loves, a love that is passion
>   And one which besides thou hast earned as thy due.
> The passionate love is the thought which forgetting
>   All else is of you, aye, for ever of you.
> Thou earnedst the other by rending asunder
>   All veils and disclosing thyself to my view.
> Not mine be the praise for the one or the other,
>   The praise and the thanks are all thine for the two."

According to Abū Ṭālib God's love resembles human affection in some respects; those whom the Divine Being loves can count on pardon when they sin. The brethren of Joseph in the Koranic narrative committed no fewer than forty offences ; yet, because they were beloved of God, all were forgiven. On the other hand, Ezra committed one offence only—he asked a question about predestination, and was erased from the list of prophets in consequence. God's love is not, however, due to anything, as human affection is due to kinship, to the possession of qualities, to the hope of advantage, etc. ; it is a free and mysterious choice from the beginning of the world. Such a mystery is known only to prophets, and to reveal it would be unbelief. Only by special revelation does a man know that he has been thus favoured; and the Ṣūfis agree with older thinkers that affliction and bereavement are a surer sign thereof than prosperity.

Unintelligible as is much of the Ṣūfi language from the abstruseness of their subject, the authors confess that there are further mysteries which either cannot or may not be revealed, and which can only be transferred from heart to heart. An example is to be found in the eighth fear, which Abū Ṭālib mentions, but dare not describe.

That the higher stages of Ṣūfism were akin to madness is not only clear of itself, but is sometimes acknowledged; Ibn 'Arabī boasts of having for a time lost his reason. A fraction of a grain of the love of God bestowed at the intercession of a saint upon an aspirant drove him mad; by renewed intercession the dose was so reduced that the aspirant recovered his reason. Ibrāhīm Ibn Adham complained of the constant mental agitation which his spiritual progress caused: he was asked in reply if he knew of any lover who was free from agitation. The attitude of the Divine Being towards these lovers is made to resemble that of the capricious beauty: the lover's attachment is kept warm by occasional frowns and neglect.   Perfect love does not cast out fear.

In the Ṣūfi poetry, as we have seen, some female name is employed as the symbol for the object of the poet's passion, and it is hard to separate this practice from the old worship of goddesses which was so prevalent among the ancient nations.   The danger of the practice was obvious: one Aḥmad Ibn 'Isā al-Kharrāz in a dream told another Ṣūfi that he had been rebuked for putting the likeness of the Divine Being on Layla and Sauda—stock-names in the erotic poetry of the Arabs.   Such verses, then, it is held, are only for those who can penetrate through the symbolism.

The close connection between music and things erotic is evinced by the history of this Ṣūfi poetry. It seems clear that music and poetry, which played so important a part in both Christian and Jewish ritual, were eschewed by the Prophet, who even delivered a polemic against the poets, though at a later period he accepted the services of a court-poet, whom he is even said to have declared inspired by the Holy Spirit.   Still, the Koran says of the Prophet, " We have not taught him versification "; and there is no place in the religious services which he instituted for hymns or odes.   The Ṣūfis, however, found that the ode had the power to remind the devotee of God, to stir his religious emotions, and they cannot therefore neglect it as a means of approaching the Deity. According to Abū Ṭālib this use of poetry goes back to Ja'far the winged, the brother of Ali who died a

12

martyr's death at Mutah and was seen by the Prophet winged in Paradise. Music was employed in the services of the days in Ramaḍān called Tashrīḳ, by the devotees of Arabia, the practice having been introduced by ʿAṭā Ibn Abī Rabāḥ. This personage kept two singing women to aid his companions in their devotions. If such a performance excites the hearer to any worldly passion, then indeed he is not entitled to listen; but if it turns his thoughts to God and excites purely spiritual longings, then he may listen with profit. To spiritual poetry of this sort the name *ḳaṣīdah*, usually used for encomium, might be employed, but not *ughniyah*, which was too suggestive of the frivolous performance which aided the toper in the enjoyment of his wine.

One other point wherein this spiritual love resembles the tender passion is that it should be concealed—kept as a secret between subject and object. If a man be asked whether he love God, he should remain silent; to deny it would be a sin, to confess it would be indecorous. Yet among the lovers some are sober, others intoxicated, and this concealment can only be expected of the former: the latter have lost all self-control and so are to be excused.

If in the Prophet's time love might be bestowed upon him as deputy for God, since his departure it may instead be bestowed on the Koran. The sacred book inherits the affection once bestowed upon the Arabian goddesses, just as with the Jews the Law gave a vent to the passion once lavished on Ashtoreth

—a curious psychological parallel. A Moslem does not merit the title "aspirant" until he finds in the Koran all that he desires. Love of the Koran is not, it would seem, quite easy to acquire. A saint asserted that he had enjoyed the Koran twenty years, but it had been a burden to him for twenty years before.

Love of God is not only incompatible with the bestowal of affection on other rational beings, but even with the most innocent enjoyments. In a revelation to Moses fault was found with a man who was perfect in every other respect, but enjoyed the morning air. Another lost rank in the spiritual world because he transferred his oratory to a tree where he could enjoy the singing of a bird. God is jealous. A devotee who had given away all he possessed asserted that this was because he had heard a human lover promising his beloved the like —sacrifice of everything; and the divine beloved can claim no less.

This road also leads to the doctrine which is so characteristic of Ṣūfism—contempt of Heaven and Hell. If God had created neither, they scornfully ask, would he be unworthy to be obeyed? Christ, according to one of their Apocrypha, passed by three sets of ascetics: a party who feared Hell; a party who hoped for Paradise; and a party whose sole motive was love of God. He reprimanded the first and second for making created things the object of their hopes and fears, and took up his abode with the third.

Still, it has to be confessed that the Koran contains
a great deal about Paradise and its sensual delights,
and that Allah therein has encouraged mankind to
look forward thereto. Hence if a man's purpose
in his service be the hope of attaining these delights,
this cannot be said to affect his sincerity and devout-
ness; for he has the highest authority for such
aspiration.[1] All that can be said is that these
persons fall short of the rank attained by the "lovers
of God"; for these persons aim at complete freedom
from every other passion but the love of God, and,
as we have seen, are indifferent to all pains and
pleasures, not excepting Heaven and Hell.

But besides the moral conclusions to be drawn
from the doctrine of the divine unity, there is also
a metaphysical conclusion; and this appears to be
the extreme attainment of the *gnosis*. The aim of
mystical speculation may be formulated as the
identification of the subject with the object; and
the name "unitarian" is mystically interpreted with
reference to this identification. The true unitarian
is he who recognises in the world no existence save
God's; who regards both himself and the world
outside him as a mirror, yet rather one wherein the
Deity shows Himself than one wherein He is re-
flected. It is conceivable that this notion may have
come into Islam from outside; on the other hand,
speculation on the doctrine of the divine unity appears sufficient to account for its development and
indeed for its origin. Had there been more gods

---

[1] Ḳ. Ḳ. ii. 151.

than one, says the Koran, the heavens and the earth must have come to grief; but if any attempt be made to define the word "god" metaphysically, speculation quickly leads to something like the truly existing or the necessarily existing; even with Homer the difference between God and man is that the former is eternal, the latter transient. The relation between God and matter immediately suggests questions: is matter independent of God, or not? The former supposition leads to polytheism, the latter only is consistent with real monotheism. If, then, God is not outside matter, He must in a way be identical with matter; and the most thoughtful of the Ṣūfis, accepting this conclusion, based on it a series of inferences as unlike the original doctrines of Islam as any that could have been evolved.

The main proposition of the esoteric Ṣūfism is, then, this—that there is no distinction between subject and object, and that God, nature, and man are identical. The consciousness of this is to be obtained through a variety of exercises, and it would seem that not everyone possesses the capacity to attain thereunto; but those who do attain thereto are apparently thought to possess divine powers. Indeed it would seem clear that when once the individual's identity with the Deity is realised he can do and will do what the Deity does. The earliest existing author who clearly formulates this theory is one Ḥallāj, who was executed in the year 922. We possess accounts of this personage by contemporaries and by others who are little later, and according to them he claimed divine powers, and even undertook to display them. He was the author of numerous works, of which a list was drawn up within a century of his death; they were thought by his enemies to be imposture. One of these treatises has recently been recovered and given to the world, called the Ṭawāsīn after a Surah of the Koran; the composition is very largely infantile, consisting of the stringing together of rhymes with very little meaning; but it is quite decided on the doctrine which has been quoted, and the famous words wherein Hallāj identified himself with God, " I am the Truth," are to be found therein. Like somewhat later mystics he divides mankind into circles, the inmost being that of the persons who attain to the consciousness of this identity with the Divine Being; and he is followed by later mystics in giving the Koran interpretations which it is clear that its author had never conceived of its bearing. In that work, naturally Iblis (Satan) and Pharaoh are quoted not as models of conduct, but as examples to be avoided; but the Ṣūfis take a different view. Hallāj reports a dialogue between himself and these two worthies, wherein they are called his masters, and the words put into their mouths in the Koran are shown to indicate the lofty stage which they had attained; when Pharaoh says he is not aware of any god for the Egyptians but himself, what he means is that he was the only person in the country who had attained to this esoteric knowledge of the identity of the creator with the created; and when Iblis or Satan declined to bow down to Adam on the ground that he had been created of fire and Adam of clay, this too is shown to have been in order.

The editor of this treatise has not furnished a translation, thinking perhaps that the time has not yet come when one could be executed with certainty ; and the infantile jingles in which it is very largely couched would render translation exceedingly difficult. It is, however, of considerable interest to have before us the actual work of the mystic who is most famous or most notorious for identifying himself with the Divine Being, and whose terrible execution is the subject of numerous descriptions and allusions ; though it would appear that it was not on account of this particular doctrine that he was condemned to a barbarous death, but because he had taught that specific performance was not requisite in the case of the pilgrimage.   It is clear from the nature of the work that it was not intended to appeal to the reason, but to the emotion, and indeed that the mode of delivery must have been of a special sort in order to compass this effect.

In a treatise which professes to be the encyclopædia of a literary society of the fourth Islamic century a threefold division of mankind is attempted with reference to their religious needs.   There is the public, *i.e.* the laity, who should be encouraged in religious exercises because they are thereby kept out of mischief ; for them all that is required is knowledge of religious ordinances, especially prayer, fasting, and alms, about which they need know no more than that they are prescribed.   A second class is constituted by what we might call the clergy, or learned clerks, *i.e.* those who make it their business to possess a scholarly acquaintance with the sources of law, so as to be able to state what the rule or approved practice is on any subject into which the code enters. But beyond this there is a third class, who occupy themselves with deeper matters: the nature and attributes of God. These are the thinkers of the community, and to a certain extent their learning must be encyclopædic; for they must be aware of the problems of providence before they can be in a position to find the answers. The problems suggested by the inequalities of nature, *e.g.* why a centipede which is so minute should require a hundred legs whereas the bulky elephant can do with four, have to be formulated first before the answer to them can be discovered ; and such formulation requires observation and, indeed, occasionally experiment. Passages could be cited from the Koran wherein reflection or speculation is highly commended ; people are bidden to think on the works of nature, and arrive at sound religious opinions in that way. In our time there are in consequence persons who assert that the physicists of Europe are the true Moslems and the traditionalists of the East heretics.

That these precepts and the belief that the highest religious stage involved encyclopædic attainments led to no real scientific progress is due to another doctrine, viz. that there was a short-cut to knowledge, *i.e.* revelation. And, quite clearly, an explanation of a difficulty furnished by the Divine Being would be far more satisfactory than the best guess which the student might make ; we philologists well know that an authoritative explanation of a passage is a far better thing than the most ingenious conjecture.   Now, the doctrine of prophecy involved the possibility that certain persons might be privileged to receive such authoritative communications.   In a Surah of the Koran we are told how Moses went about with one who had been favoured with knowledge; this personage did some very extraordinary things, which surprised and even shocked Moses ; Moses was snubbed for his inquisitiveness, but before his companion parted from him he condescended to explain his conduct.   Other prophets had been similarly favoured ; they had looked down on what seemed gross unfairness on the part of fortune, good luck coming to those who neither required nor deserved it, persons punished for offences which they had not committed ; and a divine communication had shown that the matter was of extreme simplicity.   When a man found a purse, the explanation was that the father of the loser had owed the same sum to the finder's father ; when a man was killed for an offence which he had not committed, it turned out that he was expiating his father's crime.   When some busybody endeavoured to interfere with the divine arrangements, *e.g.* by giving a blind boy his sight, the result was the upsetting of a beneficent arrangement. Whether every reader of these explanations is perfectly satisfied with the divine economy is perhaps open to question ; but there is no doubt that, supposing these explanations to be authoritative, they could not have been obtained by any amount of study.

The fundamental belief of mysticism is, then, that knowledge can be obtained in this way: communication can be established between the human being and the Divine Being, and the keys to the inner meaning of phenomena be thus obtained. It might indeed seem that such a pretension was injurious to the majesty of the Koran; for a new revelation could not well be regarded as inferior to the earlier, but should rather supersede the earlier. Some, therefore, of those who have ascribed their works to the Divine Being have endeavoured somewhat to soften or to modify this pretension; they employ some word which, though meaning the same as " revelation," is not one of the synonyms ordinarily employed in reference to the Holy Scripture; Ibn 'Arabī, though boldly pretending to an office higher than that of prophet, professes to have received his book from the Prophet Mohammed in a dream—taking care to call attention to a tradition according to which Mohammed cannot be personated in a dream by the devil, who otherwise is a quick-change artist. And in the case of a work of the fourth century of Islam, which appears to contain the genuine and undiluted mysticism, the name employed by the writer is far removed from those used of the Koran: each set of aphorisms begins, " He caused me to understand [some term] and said unto me "; where, however, the sequel shows that the speaker is the Divine Being Himself, and the commentator uses without hesitation the actual word whereby Koranic revelations are described in the sacred volume itself—"sendings down." These usually are brief aphorisms, but occasionally they extend to complicated paragraphs.

The work, like several other Arabic monuments, is regularly embedded in a commentary, of which the purpose is very often to give the opinions of the author something like an orthodox colouring. Thus the formula with which most of the aphorisms are introduced, "And he said unto me," where the pronoun is shown by the sequel to refer to the Divine Being, is explained away the first few times that it occurs: the author means that the matter was put so distinctly into his mind that it was as if the Divine Being had said unto him. Early as this work is in the series of mystic manuals, its author claims for those who are possessed of the esoteric knowledge nothing less than is claimed for them at a later time: such a person is God's viceroy on earth. For such a person religious exercises cease to have value; he is above all rules and regulations. The secret which is revealed is that God exists and nothing exists except God; the recognition of anything else except God is "association," what in the Koran is called paganism. The terms defined are largely connected with the progressive attainment of this esoteric knowledge; knowledge is expressed by three different terms, of which the intermediate appears to satisfy the writer whom we have studied so long—Abū Ṭālib al-Mekki.

The third stage, *al-wakfah*, " standing " or " under-standing," is that which constitutes the goal of the true mystic; and it is that wherein all differences between him and the Divine Being are sunk. For him neither the present nor the future world has any existence; the word " other," " besides," is banished from his vocabulary. He cannot pray: to do so would be to acknowledge that God was different from himself, and that there were things to be had other than that identity.

It is in any case a bold achievement to compose a long series of aphorisms supposed to be uttered by the Divine Being, but what must be said for al-Niffarī, the author, is that his aphorisms are profoundly earnest; they rarely suggest conscious imposture, a charge from which the work of his successor, Ibn Arabī, cannot easily be exonerated. They appear, however, to contain constant repetitions of the same thoughts in slightly different language; the imagery is at times extravagant and even grotesque; and it may often be doubted whether the propositions are meant to convey anything like their obvious meaning. But whatever be the facts about the origin of the work, it seems clear that we have in it as bold and undiluted a statement of the esoteric doctrine of the Ṣūfis as can be found. The treatises that are diluted with ethics or homilies appear to have halted half-way on the road; their authors may have themselves failed to gain admittance into the inner circle, or have been mentally unqualified for such progress. Clearly, the stage at which both devotional practice and

ascetic practice are flung aside as rudimentary discipline lies beyond that at which the one or the
other constitutes the main occupation of life.

The revelations ordinarily consist of brief aphorisms, chiefly definitions; sometimes, however, a fairly
lengthy paragraph is communicated at once, and at
times the revelation takes the form of a dialogue
between the author and the Divine Being; or instead
of a conversation there is the description of a scene.
The practical aphorisms, *i.e.* such as could be called
precepts or directions for conduct, are few in number;
and even these are seemingly contradictory. Certain
words and phrases appear to be employed in highly
technical senses, but not consistently.

What excites the wonder of the reader is that a
treatise of this sort should have been permitted to
survive, since its author makes very light of the
devotions of Islam. It would seem, however, that
among the few precepts which he receives, while that
of writing down his revelations is emphasised, some
stress is also laid on secrecy and care in the choice of
associates. Possibly he composed under an assumed
name, since the collectors of Ṣūfi biographies seem
to take no notice of him; and his commentator of
Tlemsen has not thought it worth while to give any
account of him, though he implies at times that he
was acquainted with his career, at any rate to some
extent. Nevertheless, the impression which the work
leaves on the mind is that its author knows his
business more than the other Ṣūfis of the fourth
century, *e.g.* Abū Ṭālib al-Mekki. One fancies that

he would have declared these people to have gone no further than the *gnosis*, which was only the second stage in the aspirant's course; gnosis led to understanding, which was the highest stage. The understanding is the person to whom God is revealed.

The consequence that worship is inconsistent with the state of understanding is quite fearlessly drawn. " The more the sight of God is extended, the narrower becomes the sphere of worship. When I have concentrated thy quality and thy heart upon sight of me, what hast thou to do with supplication? Shalt thou ask me to remove the veil? I have removed it. Shalt thou ask me to veil myself? Then with whom wilt thou converse? When thou hast seen me, only two petitions remain for thee: thou mayest ask me in my absence to maintain thee in my sight; and thou mayest ask me when thou seest me that thou mayest say to a thing be and it shall be. Yet I give thee leave to ask of me when I am absent. If thou canst calculate, then subtract the vision from the absence, and whichever remains over, make that prevail in the matter of petition—*i.e.* since petition is only permitted in absence, if there be more absence than presence, ask. If I am not absent when thou eatest, then I shall save thee the trouble of labouring for food. If I am not absent when thou sleepest, I shall not be absent when thou wakest. A resolve of thine to keep silence when thou seest me is a screening; how much more a resolve of thine to speak. Such resolve can only come about in absence.   To no eye or heart do I appear but I annihilate it."

The revelation dealing with the screening of the vision is rather more mysterious.   " Ignorance is the screen of vision, and knowledge is the screen of vision. I am the unscreened outside and the unrevealed interior.   Who knows the screen is near the revelation.   The screen is one, but the causes which bring it about are many.   They are the specific screens."

Just as we find that in the idealism of Kant space and time are shown to be forms of thought, *i.e.* to exist for the mind only, so our mystic thinks the same of night and day.   " Eternity worships me, and it is one of my qualities ; and out of its praise I have created the night and the day ; I have made them curtains spread out over the eyes and the thoughts, and over the hearts and over the minds.   Night and day are two curtains spread out over all that I have created, but having chosen thee for myself I have lifted those curtains in order that thou mightest see me ; and now that thou hast seen me, stand in thy station before me, and abide in the vision of me ; otherwise thou shalt be snatched by every being.   I have only raised the curtains in order that thou mightest see me, and that I might strengthen thee for the sight of the heavens splitting, and for the sight of that which descends how it descends, and that thou mightest see how that comes from my presence even as there come night and day, and all that I show unto thee."

The Kantian doctrine of space and time is ex-

pressed somewhat more distinctly in another " station,"
" Everything that is on the dust is from the dust ;
look then at the dust, and thou shalt eliminate that
which is from it ; and shalt see that which transformed
it from one individual in the sight of the eyes to
another ; thus the individuals shall not distract thee.
Take to thyself helpers for the wandering of thy gaze ;
and when thy gaze no longer wanders then no helpers
are required. The dispensing with helpers shall not
be until there is no time ; and there shall be no time
only when there are no individuals ; and there shall
be no individuals only when thou seest them not, but
seest me."

[The aspirant, then, is to direct his thoughts to
the matter and the power which transforms it into
different substances and individuals ; this transformation takes place in time ; and only when the aspirant
has forgotten the individual existences, and realised
only the transforming power, can he do without
helpers, *i.e.* the ascetic practices which will enable
him to reach what is behind phenomena.]

The following " station " deals with " vicinity," *i.e.*
what is meant by being " near God," an epithet
which in the Koran is applied to a favoured class,
which includes the Christian Saviour. It is shown
that the notions of distance and vicinity in this context have nothing to do with space.

" He caused me to understand *vicinity,* and said to
me : Nothing is further from me than any other
thing, and nothing is nearer to me than any other
thing, except as I institute its nearness or farness.

" Distance is known to thee by vicinity, and vicinity is known to thee by sensation ; the most elementary acquaintance with vicinity is thy perceiving the trace of my sight in everything, so that this affects thee more than thy knowledge [of the thing].

" The vicinity which thou knowest, as compared with the vicinity which I know, is like thy knowledge compared with my knowledge.

" Neither my vicinity nor my distance is known to thee, nor my description according as it really is.

" I am the near, yet not as one thing is near another ; and the distant, yet not as one thing is distant from another.

" Thy nearness and thy farness are not thine ; it is I that am the near and the distant, whose nearness is distance and whose distance is nearness.

" The nearness and the distance which thou knowest are measured by space ; but I am near and distant without space.

" I am nearer to the tongue than its utterance, when it utters ; whoso witnesses me makes no mention, and whoso mentions me witnesses not.

" He who witnesses and mentions, if what he witnesses be not real is screened by what he mentions.

" I make myself known to thee and thou knowest me not—that is distance ; thy heart sees me, yet sees me not—that is distance ; thou perceivest me, yet perceivest me not—that is distance. Thou describest me, yet not according to my description—that is distance. Thou hearest my addressing thee from thy heart, whereas the address is from me—that is distance ; thou seest thyself, whereas I am nearer to thee than thy sight—that is distance."

The following is an account of the main doctrine, but rather obscurely and mysteriously expressed :

" Thou must not go out of thy house save unto me ; thou shalt then be in my protection, and I shall be thy helper.

" I am God ; thou canst not enter unto me by bodies, nor perceive my knowledge by fancies.

" Whatsoever thou seest with thine eye and thy heart of the realm of the manifest and the secret, and whose submission unto me and humiliation before me, and before the majesty of my might, I have made thee witness through some knowledge which I have established for thee, which thou knowest by witnessing, not by expression—beyond that knowledge I have made thee pass, and from other infinite cognisances and the tongues of their utterers, and have opened unto thee therein my gates which are only entered by him whose knowledge is strong enough to sustain the knowledge of them, so that thou sustainest them and not they thee ; by reason of what I have made thee witness of them, and not permitted them to witness of thee ; and so thou hast reached the bound of the Presence, and the arrival of one and another has been announced : thereupon reflect who thou art and whence thou hast entered, and what thou didst know so that thou couldst enter, and why thou didst hear so that thou couldst sustain.

" When I shall cause thee to witness every exist-ence at once, in one vision, then at that station I have certain forms, which if thou knowest, invoke me by them ; but if thou knowest them not, then invoke me by the pain of this vision in thy troubles.

" The description of this vision is that thou shouldst see the height and the depth and the length and the breadth, and all that is therein, and all whereby that is in what is manifest and abiding and subjected and striving, and shouldst witness the existence of each returning its gaze towards itself, since each particular thereof cannot advance except towards its parts, and shouldst witness the places thereof whereon the eye falls, wherein existence establishes its hymnody directed towards me with the eulogies of its praise, staring at me with the glory-giving which distracts it from everything else than its continuance in its devotions ; then when thou seest [the existences] with their faces [so] turned, say : O thou who conquerest everything by the appearance of thy sovereignty, and who appropriatest everything by the despotism of thy might, thou art the Powerful who canst not be resisted, and canst not be described ; and when thou witnessest them staring in order to give glory, then say : O merciful, O pitying One ; 1 ask thee by thy mercy whereby thou hast established in thy knowledge and strengthened and elevated unto thy mention and raised the minds unto yearning after thee, and whereby thou hast ennobled the station of whom thou wilt among thy creatures before thee.

" Knowledge is what thou feelest, but the realisation of knowledge is what thou dost witness.

" Is not the fact that I have sent unto thee the

sciences from the direction of thy heart a withdrawing of thee from the general to the special? Is not my privileging thee by making myself known to thee, so that thou canst abandon thy heart and the sciences which have appeared to thee, revelation? Does not revelation mean that thou shouldst banish from thee everything and the knowledge of everything, and witness me in that which I have made thee witness? So that no alarmer alarms thee at that time, neither does any companion cheer thee, whilst I make thee witness and make myself known unto thee, though it were but once in thy lifetime; telling thee that thou art my friend, inasmuch as thou dost negate everything by virtue of what I have made thee witness, so that I become the controller of thee, and thou comest between me and everything, and thou art attached to me, whilst everything [else] is attached to thee, not to me. And this is the description of my friends, and know that thou art my friend, and that thy knowledge is the knowledge of my friendship. So commit unto me thy name that I may meet thee therewith, and set between me and thee no name nor knowledge, and discard all names and sciences which I display unto thee owing to the majesty of my vision, lest thou thereby be screened from me.

"Everything has its sorcery, and the sorcery of the letters is the names; depart from the names, thou shalt depart from the meanings.

"He caused me to understand the command, and said unto me: Execute what I command thee and wait not for cognisance; verily if thou wait for cognisance of my command thou shalt disobey my command.

" If thou dost not execute my command until the cognisance thereof appears to thee, thou obeyest the cognisance of the command, not the command.

" Knowest thou what it is which stops thee from executing my command and wait for the cognisance thereof?   It is thy soul, which seeks knowledge that she may be superior to my decrees, and that she may go by her own guidance in its paths.   Verily cognisance has ways, the ways valleys, the valleys outlets and highroads, and the highroads difference of direction.

" Execute my command when I command thee, and ask not concerning the cognisance thereof; even so those that are in my presence, the angels of the decrees, carry out what they are commanded and make no inquiries; execute without inquiry, and thou shalt be of me and I of thee.

" It is not out of grudging that I conceal from thee cognisance of the command; only cognisance is that station of wisdom which I have set for thee; and if I assent to thy cognisance of anything, I command thee to abide there; and if thou abide not there, thou disobeyest me, because I have made cognisance a judgment, and when I show thee a cognisance, I command thee to judge thereby.

" If I command thee, and thy intellect come and intervene, then banish it, and if thy heart come and intervene, then dismiss it, so thou mayest execute my command, and let nothing else accompany thee ; for then thou shalt advance therein ; but if anything else accompany thee, then it will cause thee to stop short of it, for thy intellect will stay thee until thou knowest, and only when it knows does it give preference, and thy heart will stay thee, and when it knows it will favour."

The next translation is of a highly mystical passage :

" Instruction of the Sea.

" He caused me to understand the sea, and I beheld the boats sinking but the planks escaping. Then the planks sank, and he said unto me, None who sails escapes. He risks his life who flings himself therein and sails not. He perishes who sails and risks not ; in risking there is some safety ; for the wave comes and raises what is beneath it, and it sinks upon the shore. The surface of the sea is a light that cannot be attained owing to the distance of its path, and its bed is darkness that cannot be endured ; and between the two are monsters from which no one is secure. Sail not on the sea lest I screen thee by the instrument ; and fling not thyself therein lest I screen thee therewith. In the sea are bounds, and which of them shall support thee ? If thou givest thyself to the sea and art drowned therein, thou shalt be like one of its creatures. I should deceive thee if I pointed thee towards any but thyself. If thou perish in aught beside me thou shalt remain even as thou hast perished therein. The world is for him whom I have diverted from it and from whom I have diverted it ; and the next world is for him towards whom I have advanced it, together with myself."

It appears from these quotations that the mysticism of Islam is developed on lines of its own, and has only a superficial resemblance to other sorts. Its goal, Fanā, " perdition," means losing consciousness of all other existences besides that of God ; and this goal seems so clearly suggested by the Koranic doctrine that nothing should be associated with God, that we may even doubt the influence of India, which in its philosophy of Maya or " delusion " seems often to run on parallel lines.' The problem of Indian philosophy is, however, a different one, being suggested by the doctrine of transmigration ; how is the soul, constantly shifting from one embodiment to another, to attain rest ? The problem of Islamic mysticism is: how is the Moslem to fulfil the command to associate nothing with God ? He fulfils it in the first place by banishing from his mind all desires except the desire for God ; by rejecting and contemning earthly joys first, and then heavenly joys : and since Paradise has no attraction for him, he speedily arrives at the conclusion that the ceremonial performances by which it is to be earned can have only disciplinary, at most sacramental, value. But he is then faced with the difficulty that his senses in the first place and his intelligence in the second tell him of other things existing besides God ; of various phænomena and noümena. He must then somehow or other eliminate these also ; and finally eliminate himself, because he must not treat himself as different from God, since otherwise he will be no complete monotheist.

Now, what appears from the treatise whence these extracts have been taken is that the author endeavours to set forth matters of experience, propositions which perhaps convey a meaning to one who has gone through a certain training, but which are most imperfectly understood by others : and it may be gathered that even with himself the consciousness was not persistent, but occasional. But just as with the Indian philosophies the goal was the same, though the methods were variable, so with the Moslem mystics the end was definite, though different sects and orders supposed it could be attained by somewhat different modes of procedure. Philanthropy and social reform seem, however, to have been rather by-products of the movement than to have constituted an essential part of it. The essential thing is salvation, for which, curiously enough, a term signifying perdition is employed.

Of sacred literature outside the region of Islam, it is probable that parts of the Fourth Gospel bear the closest resemblance which can be found to the esoteric Ṣūfism ; a question not easily answered is whether we have independent products before us, or whether the thoughts of Niffarī are directly inherited from the author of the Christian work.

LECTURE VII

As "a detailed account of everything" the Koran might reasonably be expected to give clear and satisfactory answers to those questions which come within religious metaphysics, *e.g.* responsibility, and the nature of the soul and of God. Possibly a consistent system on these subjects is scarcely attainable; and one of even ostensible consistency can only be devised by patient study and purely objective speculation. The Prophet's busy and active life neither favoured nor even permitted such processes; whence, when these questions became troublesome, they had to be answered as best suited the immediate need. Thus the Prophet's first and main message appears to have been to warn his countrymen of an approaching Day of Judgment, accompanied by the resurrection of the dead; and, like the ancient Pharisees and Sadducees, he and they appear to have differed on the question whether the dead are or are not to rise. It seems, however, clear that if the dead are to rise in order to be judged, Paradise and Hell cannot follow immediately upon death; the ultimate condition indicated by those two words must come after Judgment, not before. Until, then, Moslems fought battles wherein they slew Unbelievers and were themselves slain, there was little difficulty in making the dead unconsciously await the final trump, when they were to be raised for judgment; but the first of the Moslem battles rendered such delay intolerable. The martyrs had to enter Paradise at once, and the dead Unbelievers had immediately to be convinced of their error. Nevertheless, the doctrine of the Day of Judgment was too deeply interwoven with Islam — being mentioned in the familiar prayer which afterwards was placed at the commencement of the Koran—to be abandoned. Since men's natural beliefs on these subjects are inconsistent and contradictory, possibly the Koran is not thereby the less suited to the religious needs of the community; just as the inconsistencies in the Homeric and Vergilian Infernos are assuredly what constitute their beauty and their truth. But when it is desirable to extract dogma, in order to know precisely what is to be believed, and to penalise those who hold erroneous opinions, such inconsistency is exceedingly troublesome.

Now the word Metaphysics means " after physics," and it seems clear that it is only after some progress has been made with the physical sciences that metaphysical questions can be profitably studied. For founding despotisms no particular knowledge of either appears to be requisite; but when an empire has to be maintained on a religious basis, systematisation becomes necessary, and the studies which should have preceded the composition of the sacred book cannot be permanently kept out. It was not, then, the variant readings of the Koran, but the rough-and-ready nature of its composition, which necessarily brought about sectarianism. And in the opinion of competent authorities the sect which comes nearest to the original Islam is not one of those whose adherents can be counted by millions, but one of which there are scanty relics in corners of Arabia, Algeria, and the Tripolitaine, whose very name suggests " going out," not remaining within the fold.

The scientific and philosophical level of the Koran appears, then, to be but slightly, if at all, superior to that of the pagan Arabs; it recommends the study and observation of nature, but the author clearly had no idea that nature had ever been methodically studied, and his own observations are elementary. The sun rises over people who are without shelter from it, and sinks into a muddy well or a hot spring —for it is uncertain how the passage should be read; the mountains serve as pillars to prevent the earth from swaying; domestic animals are of four sorts—sheep, oxen, goats, and camels. There are two seas, one sweet and the other salt ; there is a barrier between them which prevents their mixing. The shooting stars are flames aimed at rebellious jinn who eavesdrop at the heavenly council. Though the existence of other gods than Allah is vehemently denied, nevertheless these non-existent beings will repudiate their worshippers on the Day of Judgment. Birds and insects not only are credited with uttering the praises of God, which might well be regarded as a poetical expression, but they are introduced into narratives as reasoning and speaking, in a way which has since given serious trouble ; it has been argued from the Koran that even mountains probably have thought and reason, but for some cause have ordinarily been deprived of speech, and that beasts and birds are responsible agents. So we fancy that the doctrine of the Koran according to which Unbelievers' hearts are as hard as stone or even harder has led to the belief that this is physically the case. The historian Ṭabarī gravely records how, when the heart of the insurgent Shabīb was taken out, it rebounded as high as a man's stature when flung on the ground, so hard-hearted was this insurgent.[1]

Since the Koran claims to give an exhaustive account of everything, it was probably entirely against the Prophet's wish that it should be supplemented by any other sort of knowledge, and his attitude even to the poets was hostile. As we have repeatedly seen, the existence of the Koran in his time was more like that of a running stream than of an accumulated mass ; if difficulties arose, they could be solved by the summary process of erasing one verse and substituting another. There is much homily, but no dogmatic-system ; even on the question whether the beings worshipped in addition to Allah have any existence the Koran is self-contradictory ; if they are merely names coined by your ancestors, they will not be in a position to repudi-

____
[1] ii. 976.

ate their worshippers. On the question whether all Moslems will be saved or whether only Moslems will be saved, there are similarly contradictory statements: varying according to the Prophet's mood or political needs. By the end of three centuries we find a very different state of affairs. All these questions have been posed and a definite reply given as the orthodox answer; in the treatise of Abu'l-Ḥasan al-Ash‘arī, which bears date about that time, we have a series of results which to this day are accepted as the dogma of Islam by the bulk of its adherents.

Now, it is noticeable that the literature called Arabian philosophy is mostly later than this date ; the chief translators of Greek philosophical works and the chief reproductions of those treatises belong to the fourth, fifth, and sixth centuries. The discussions whereby the ultimate orthodoxy was evolved therefore took place at a period earlier than the wholesale introduction of Greek philosophy into Moslem countries. When it was introduced in this fashion it had the reputation of unorthodoxy ; to possess the works of Aristotle or of Avicenna was rarely safe ; philosophers were denounced from the pulpit, and pious sovereigns made holocausts of their works. Hence the influence of Greek thought in building up the dogmatics of Islam, though considerable, is likely to have been in the main indirect.

The works in which the few great thinkers of mankind have stated their views are in most cases difficult ; what suits the public far more is some compendium or summary. In our time the number of persons who have read the *Origin of Species* bears no proportion to the number of Darwinians; and similarly in ancient times the number of persons whose thoughts were guided by the discoveries of Plato and Aristotle vastly exceeded that of those who had read their works, or, indeed, heard their names. Prior to the rise of Islam translations of Greek philosophical works had been issued in the languages of the nations which shortly after its rise were to be incorporated in its empire—the Syrians and the Persians; but the ideas of the Greeks had been current among the peoples with whom the Arabs associated long before. Uneducated as was the author of the Koran, it is clear that even that work contains traces of Aristotelian thought. When Satan refuses to bow down before Adam on the ground that he had been created of fire, whereas Adam had been created of clay, the underlying thought is that of Aristotle's Physics: wherein the proof is given that fire is more honourable than earth, because in the hierarchy of the elements fire is at the top, whereas earth is at the bottom. Similarly, though the Prophet is unlikely to have heard of the *Odyssey*, we are justified in finding an allusion to Penelope in the woman who undid her spinning after it had been wound.[1] Such discoveries as Aristotle's analysis of the reasoning process become common property, and influence the thought of persons who are quite unacquainted with their origin; but that

[1] Surah xvi. 94.

origin not having been forgotten, under certain conditions persons are likely to arise who will go back to the source.

Towards the end of the second century there arose sovereigns who had a genuine desire to possess accurate translations of Greek philosophical masterpieces; and when such translations were published, there were Moslems who studied them with great care. A philosopher of the early third century is charged with substituting for the Koran Aristotle's Physics, *de Generatione et Corruptione*, and Logic; with spending his time on those studies, and neglecting his fasts.[1] One of the friends of Jāḥiẓ, who lived at that time, had a slave-girl who had mastered the whole of Euclid, whereas some Moslem men were unable to master a single proposition.[2] In the middle of the third century the study of Greek geometry is recommended as necessary for the sharpening of the intellect, and there were both Christian and Moslem teachers of it. The ultra - orthodox regarded it as heretical and dangerous.[3] There is reason for thinking that even towards the end of the first century Greek authorities on various forms of the black art had obtained access to the Moslem court. But the doctrine that only the Koran might be studied, which, as we have seen, at first prevailed, probably would not have given way except to so tremendous a breach in the continuity of Islam as was brought about by the transference

---

[1] Mukhtalif al-Ḥadīth, p. 67.   [2] Ḥayawān i. 28.
[3] Yāḳūt ii. 45.

of the capital to the new city on the Tigris, and the consequent inheritance by the Caliphs of the traditions of the old Persian kings. Baghdad, growing with phenomenal rapidity, speedily attracted to itself all that was in any sense remarkable in the Islamic empire. Shāfiʻī, who lived in the second half of the second century, when the city was still new, said that Baghdad was the world;[1] all else was the country, or, as he expressed it, the desert. He who had not seen Baghdad had not seen mankind. It was there that Moslem literature began, and this also grew no less rapidly than the city; there were authors of the third century whose volumes might be counted by the hundred or more. Much of their matter was either derived from or suggested by translations from other languages. But the main lines of Moslem heresies had been marked out before the foundation of that metropolis, whence the influence of philosophy upon them must, as has been seen, have been indirect, *i.e.* due to those results which had become the common property of mankind.

For lack of any other matter to be read the first Moslems conned the Koran; and since political meetings could be explained to the authorities as Bible-classes, it is probable that gatherings for the study of the sacred volume were no less common than private study. The sects, called by the orthodox "the people of fancies," when they had no intention of breaking with Islam, found in the sacred volume the basis of their systems; even the doctrine that Ali

---

[1] Ḳ. Ḳ. ii. 49.

was an incarnation of the divine being, held by a sect called the Sabā'īs, whom Ali himself condemned to the stake, could and probably did cite a text of the Koran wherein the adjective Ali, " sublime," is applied to Allah. The fanatics called Khawārij, whose main doctrine was that the evil-doer was an Unbeliever, and that in consequence the subject had a right to revolt against a monarch who did wrong, were firm upholders of the Koran. When they split into parties, one maintaining that the wives and children of the unorthodox (in their sense) should be massacred, the other disapproving of this course, each party based its case on Koranic texts. There is no reason for supposing that they did otherwise than follow their lights ; but very much depended on the texts which they treated as " The Mother of the Book," *i.e.* the principles according to which the other texts should be interpreted. As they studied the sacred volume questions of all sorts suggested themselves to the intelligent ; and the origin of all the sects appears to have been discoveries made by the pious in the course of their perusal.

Our authorities would have us believe that the discussion of religious metaphysics went back even to the Prophet's time, and quote his opinions on the subject of sects which, we fancy, cannot in his day have had any conscious or recognised existence. But though these stories appear to be fables, we cannot easily shake the evidence which ascribes to many of the sects very high antiquity. A man who was born in the year 9 A.H., and whose mother was charged with acting as mischief-maker between the Prophet's wives, and was executed by him in consequence, is said to have been an adept in the arguments of the Mu'tazils or believers in the freedom of the will, to which sect he belonged.[1] Our earliest collection of traditions, the author of which died in the year 179, contains a saying of the Prophet concerning these heretics; and the pious Caliph O'mar II., who died just at the end of the first century of Islam, is quoted in the same collection as consulting a jurist on the subject of the same heretics, and agreeing that the right course to pursue with them was to summon them to repent, and, in the event of their declining, to put them to the sword.[2] It is difficult to reject the story, since the jurist consulted by Omar II. was the uncle of Mālik himself. And before the first half of the third century was finished, the refutation of heretics had become a familiar subject.[3]

If we may believe the chronicles, the theory of the pious Omar II. that Believers in the Freedom of the Will should be summoned to repent, and in case of their refusing should be put to death, was actually put in force by his successors. The act whereby his successor Hishām was most likely to win the favour of God was, according to one of his contemporaries, that he slaughtered or banished these heretics.[4] A specimen of his method is recorded. One Ghailan had made himself conspicuous as a heresiarch. He is summoned to the presence of the Caliph, and con-

---

[1] Aghānī xvii. 95.　　　　　　[2] Muwaṭṭa, ed. Zurḵānī, iii. 83.

[3] Jāḥiẓ, Ḥayawān i. 93.　　　　[4] Ṭabarī ii. 1777.

fronted with an orthodox theologian.   He asks:
Does God will that He should be disobeyed?   The
orthodox theologian replies by a counter-question:
Is God disobeyed against His will?   Ghailan hesi-
tates for a reply; and the Caliph orders his hands
and feet to be amputated.   During the second
century, though the third Yazīd, whose reign was
ephemeral, belonged to the Kadaris or Believers in
the Freedom of the Will, and chose a successor in
accordance with his co-religionists' advice, this sect
remained highly unpopular; to say a man belonged
to it was in the year 126 sufficient to make the mob
tear him in pieces.[1]   A jurist who died in 198
formulated the opinion that one who asserted the
Creation of the Koran—a shibboleth of the sect—
should be decapitated and his body thrown into the
Tigris.[2]

It will be seen from this that the record of Islam
for religious persecution in the case of sects which all
claimed to be Mohammedan at times by no means
fell short of that which characterised mediæval
Christianity.   And neither the Umayyads nor the
Abbasids were specially notorious for fanaticism.   A
historian of the sects who writes early in the fifth
century tells us that by then sectarianism had
acquired a sort of legal status.   The sectarian was to
be allowed to be buried in a Moslem cemetery; he
was to receive his share of the booty in war; and he
was to be allowed to pray · in a mosque.   On the
other hand, no prayer was to be said over him or

<hr>

[1] Tabarī ii. 1828.   [2] Tabakāt al-Huffāz i. 302.

behind him; food slaughtered by him was to be unlawful; nor was there to be any *jus connubii* between him and the orthodox.[1] In some ways, then, the heretic was to be inferior to the Jew or Christian, in others superior. Some rulers assimilated them altogether to the tolerated cults.[2]

What strikes us as noteworthy in the case of the particular heresy called Kadariyyah, or belief in the freedom of the will, is that unlike some others its connection with politics appears to have been slight. Where the heretic disallowed the claim of a sovereign, the reasons for persecuting him were obvious; for no reliance could be placed on his allegiance. He was a member of a conspiracy against the existing regime. But persecution merely on account of dogma unconnected with politics is less easy to understand in the case of a system which to some extent tolerated disagreement with itself.

In several other cases the supposed inventors of heretical opinions are placed at dates which seem to exclude their having been directly influenced by Greek philosophy. The origins of theological discussions are connected by the historians not with discussions with Unbelievers, but with the civil wars which broke out fiercely before the jubilee of the Migration. The fact clearly appeared that persons whose antecedents would argue a high degree of saintliness were found in opposing camps. The Prophet's favourite wife went to war with the husband of the Prophet's daughter, and the foremost

---

[1] 'Abd al-Ḳāhir, p. 11.   [2] Letters of Ḵhwārizmī.

champion of Islam.   What was forcibly brought home by these events was that " Believer " and " virtuous " could scarcely be regarded as convertible terms : for on the one hand it would be hard to deny that Ali and ʿĀ'ishah were Believers ; on the other hand, where parties resort to the decision of the battle-field, they are intentionally aiming at each other's death.   The Koran is so emphatic in its making Hell-Fire the eternal doom of one who intentionally kills a Believer,[1] that these civil wars occasioned the gravest theological difficulties to those who regarded the Book as infallible.   On the one hand, these heroes and heroines were certainly Believers : on the other hand, they had certainly led armies against Believers and left some slain on the field.   The question how far their future, and indeed their status in this life, was affected by their having aimed at the unpardonable offence of compassing the death of Moslems suggested itself at once.   And the individual who is perhaps most usually regarded as the founder of Muʿtazilism, and whose death is placed in the year 131, *i.e.* just at the termination of the Umayyad period, made what might seem a valuable suggestion for dealing with this difficulty.   By capital offences the Moslem did not, as the sect called Khārijīs ordinarily taught, become an Unbeliever ; he entered an intermediate state, in which he forfeited his claim to the title Believer without earning the other.   And this opinion was regarded as characteristic of the school.

[1] iv. 92.

The name " Mu'tazil," by which this school is most commonly known, is identical with the word for "neutral," used repeatedly of those who kept out of the civil wars and sided with neither party.[1] The name may then in origin be a political one; more probably, however, it is taken from a passage in the Koran where Abraham says he will keep away or withdraw from the pagans and what they associate with God. The Mu'tazils are otherwise known to have called themselves the " people of monotheism and justice." By justice they meant that in their system God escaped the charge of ordaining that men should disobey Him and punishing them for doing so; but their claim to monotheism is less clear, since their opponents could with some show of justice call them the Mazdians of Islam, inasmuch as they postulated a power that was co-ordinate with God, or at any rate restricted the arbitrary power which the others assigned Him. It does not seem possible to look for the source of these and similar names outside Islam with any chance of success; whence it would appear that the problems originated in the study of the sacred volume, which professed to contain the answer to all questions on all subjects, and certainly approaches this particular problem more than once. What we are at liberty to suppose is that some help for pursuing the study was obtained from outside, just as some suggestions for the grammatical study of the Koran were certainly obtained from Syrians, though never acknowledged.

[1] Ṭabarī i. 3342, 4, 9; 3427, etc.

Here, too, as in the case of jurisprudence, the debate precedes the treatise. The mosques, where any teacher could form his circle, served as debating-rooms, where questions could be asked and opinions be formulated.

One of those who attended these discussions has left us a notice of some that he heard. The questioning reminds us of the Socratic dialogues; the able questioner could reduce the opponent to silence. The Mu‘tazils asserted that the epithet "hearing" applied to the Deity meant "knowing"; the Koranic text was quoted: "Verily God has heard the speech of those who said," and the question was asked: Had God heard it before they said it? The reply was in the negative. But did God know it before they said it? The reply was affirmative. The questioner then asked whether that did not prove that the word "hear" in this text meant something other than know? To this no answer could be given. The reporter of this debate says that he asked these reasoners why when they were thus convicted of error they did not revise their opinions, since they all claimed that reason should be followed whithersoever it led. He was told that if they allowed themselves to be convinced they would find themselves changing their opinions many times a day. The hearer's conclusion was naturally very unfavourable to the debaters, since they were not advancing upon a scientific road, but merely defending shibboleths; and he held with some show of justice that it was better in that case to follow the opinions of the ancients, and especially the traditions of the Prophet. And he urges with some reason against the philosophical schools that their results exhibit no consistency; the various sects of Mu'tazils charge each other with unbelief just as the orthodox charge them all with it. Yet in the case of the real sciences everyone says the same. All calculators are agreed as to their sums; all physicians are agreed as to the treatment of the same maladies.

Nevertheless, it is probable that these debates were far from ineffective, at any rate in guiding opinion and winning adherents. In the story quoted the narrator ascribes his own conversion to orthodoxy to his witnessing the nonplussing of a Mu'tazil. And since Mu'tazilism represents at least to a moderate extent freedom of thought, it is not unnatural that the ablest Moslem thinkers of the early centuries belonged to one of its branches. Indeed, in the biography of Abu'l-Ḥasan al-Ash'arī, who has the reputation of having won the case for orthodoxy, it is granted that the orthodox could not ordinarily produce any debater who could hold his own against the Mu'tazils. The biographer supposes that the temporary victory of Mu'tazilism in the early third century was owing to the fact that the orthodox party produced martyrs, but not debaters; not because the orthodox were incompetent reasoners, but because they regarded it as improper to talk to the unorthodox or share a carpet with them. Abu'l-Ḥasan al-Ash'arī, having, indeed, special authorisation, overcame this prejudice and defeated the unorthodox on their own ground. Nevertheless, there was occasional recrudescence of Mu'tazil opinions. One of the most famous of ministers and scholars, the Ṣāḥib Ibn 'Abbād, belonged to their school. In the fifth century a vizier of the Seljuk Sultan, who followed the same system, was strong enough to introduce the practice of cursing the name of Abu'l-Ḥasan al-Ash'arī in the Friday sermon, an honour which had once fallen to Ali ; and even to start a general persecution of Ash'arites, which was shortly afterwards followed by a counter-persecution, when an orthodox vizier had been installed.   It is not in favour of these supposed freethinkers that, on the occasions when they obtained political power, they should have exhibited gross intolerance towards their opponents ; but it is a mistake to suppose that in this matter one sect is much better than another.

That the philosophical study of the Koran, in the sense of free speculation on its doctrines and their ostensible basis, would lead some minds to scepticism and even atheism might be expected *a priori* ; but naturally such conclusions as these were ordinarily so dangerous that the inquirers would keep them to themselves.   It is, indeed, asserted by the historian of the sects that the Carmathians, or, as he calls them, the *Bāṭinis*, who for some fifty years were the terror of the pilgrims, were actually atheists ; and he quotes a letter supposed to be addressed by one of their leaders to another, in which the prophets and their codes are criticised in the style to which we are accustomed in the publications of the Rational Press

Association.   Mohammed in particular is made out
to have been a shrewd adventurer who persuaded his
followers to pay ready money in the shape of their
goods and lives, while he postponed payment which
was to take the form of the Garden of Delight.   This
sect, he asserts, declared Paradise was to be found in
this world only, and, indeed, in the shape of sensual
pleasures; Hell, on the other hand, was to be found
in the religious observances which the Moslem code
enjoined.   This society, which had secret agents in
various parts of the Moslem world, endeavoured to
win followers by playing on the weakness of the
particular Moslem with whom they came in contact,
and, having found somewhere a rift in his orthodoxy,
endeavoured to widen it.   Of course we cannot
accept the account of the system given by an enemy,
who acknowledges that it was esoteric, not revealed
except to persons who, after probation, and before it
was disclosed to them, were made to swear that they
would not reveal it; but his quotations from their
literature at any rate show that there were persons
even in the early centuries of Islam who had the
hardihood to break away from the Koran, without
substituting any other form of revelation for it.

The great bulk of the sects, however, by no means
did this.   They all accepted the sacred book as of
paramount authority, and quoted it in defence of all
their dogmas.   And a Christian polemical writer has
with justice called attention to the inconsistency of the
Shī‘ah in accepting the Koran as genuine when it was
known to have been collected by sovereigns whom

they brand as wicked usurpers, who did not even accept the copy which Ali possessed as orthodox. Probably greater inconveniences would result if they were to abandon it. And it is probable that all accepted the miracle of the Koran, in some sense or other. The difficulty, however, of treating the literary style as miraculous was found appalling, and many had to retreat on the miracle which lay in the matter which the Prophet communicated being unknown to him through any ordinary channels ; but even this doctrine involved implicit belief in the accuracy of tradition, which many thinkers impugned. Indeed, when the controversy of Islam was practically closed, towards the beginning of its fourth century, free-thinking was identified with the abandonment of tradition. The theologian who finally won the case for what has since been orthodoxy, Abu'l-Ḥasan al-Ash'arī, after having for forty years been un-orthodox—a Mu'tazil,—was visited by the Prophet in a dream, who told him to undertake the defence of the sunnah ; and in consequence this theologian made a pile of the metaphysical works which he possessed, and returned to the study of tradition. He mounted the pulpit in the mosque of Baṣrah, divested himself of his robe, and declared that he divested himself of his errors in the same way.

The fact that the command which he received from the Prophet was to *write books* in defence of orthodoxy shows a considerable advance during these three hundred years in controversial methods. The command which the Prophet himself received and delivered was to compel agreement by far more forcible methods.

Since the time of this personage, Abu'l-Ḥasan al-Ash'arī, orthodox Islam is called after his name; the Sunnites should also be Ash'arites. Not all his three hundred works appear to be preserved; but one which contains an epitome of his controversies exists, and has recently been printed at Hyderabad. Orthodox theology after his time largely consists in defending his opinions; and the increasing knowledge of Greek philosophy which subsequent centuries brought caused further objections to be raised, and some fresh solutions of metaphysical puzzles to be invented. His manuals, as often happens, gave way to newer compendia of the system. Yet the dogmas formulated by him appear to have remained unaltered; and from his time the number of recognised sects seems scarcely to have been increased. The study of sectarian opinions and of the correct mode of dealing with them gradually stereotyped into an unalterable science.

The examination of the ideas which went to make up Islam did not, then, commence with the period of written literature, but rather that written literature represents the outcome of the studies of a hundred and twenty years, if we date from the time when the Koran was completed and assumed its ultimate form. Since that work claimed to give an explanation of everything, as each philosophical question was posed the students searched the sacred volume to discover what its reply was; and it clearly was made to reply to questions which had not been asked of its author. A question which occupied the Greek philosophers was whether the non-existent could be said to be. And according to our answer to that question we shall decide whether creation means making out of nothing, or making out of something. The Koran is found to reply to this question when the Deity says to Zachariah, "We created thee before when thou wast nothing."

Against this simple answer it would also be possible to quote the sacred volume for the assertion that man was created from clay, and it could scarcely be asserted that clay was nothing. And this phenomenon being found in the case of practically every controversy, one possible method of obtaining a peaceful solution was to admit that both parties were right. And this view was actually maintained by one philosopher, 'Ubaidallah b. al-Ḥasan, who was ḳāḍī or judge of Baṣrah in the year 158 A.H., and therefore early among the metaphysical speculators. He found the Koran contained texts which were in favour of free will, and others in favour of fatalism: he held that both views were correct. He thought a Moslem adulterer might be called an unbeliever or a believer or a hypocrite or a pagan; since all these titles might be justified from the sacred volume, they were all correct. With regard to the wilful murderer of a Moslem, you would be correct in holding that he was saved or that he was damned or that his fate was undecided. His meaning was thought to be that, since all these opinions appeared to be found in the Koran, he had been ordered to believe in them all ; and it was not for him to claim any further knowledge.[1] There were persons who endeavoured to settle the controversy on the creation of the Koran in the same satisfactory way, by allowing that both views might be held. Naturally, this attitude would not suit many minds, and it is doubtful whether this personage had even the honour of founding a school.

It seems doubtful whether the most freethinking among the philosophers displayed a more tolerant spirit towards unbelievers than did the orthodox ; there are, however, some signs that occasionally their reasoning too led them to propositions which would involve a completer tolerance than was usually exhibited. As we have seen, the orthodox view is that the unbeliever's acts do not count ; the one iniquity of which he can be found guilty is that of having neglected to study the evidences of Islam. Abu'l-Hudhail found an ingenious argument whence it appeared that the unbeliever did perform certain acts that are pleasing to God. For the word of God contains commands and prohibitions, and to obey a prohibition is to obey a command. Now, the Koran declares that Islam is the only religion in God's eyes, and so forbids all other religions. If, then, the unbeliever followed all the forbidden cults, he would be disobeying without obeying ; but since he follows one cult, and eschews the rest, by the mere fact of his following one forbidden cult he obeys the command with regard to all the other

----

[1] Mukhtalif al-Ḥadīth, p. 57.

forbidden cults. The reply to this ingenious argument is got from the observation of Aristotle that a thing may have more than one contrary; whence it may be possible to violate a false religion without thereby obeying the true one.

One of the philosophers took the view that all non-Moslems would, instead of being punished in the next world, merely turn into dust; his theory being that knowledge was obligatory, *i.e.* it could not be acquired but came by compulsion; those therefore to whom knowledge had not come were irresponsible, and could have no future life. Another philosopher, himself, it is said, the son of a captive, disapproved of captivity, *i.e.* of making slaves; his argument is not perfectly clear, but he evidently assumes that captives will be non-Moslems who had as yet no knowledge of God, and who therefore had committed no offence justifying their being made captives. This voice against slavery is almost the only one we can find in Islamic literature; and it wins so little accord in the orthodox critic's mind that the latter proudly argues from it that the author of this doctrine, being himself the son of a captive and slave-girl, thereby demonstrates his own illegitimacy; for according to his own doctrine his father had no right to possess a slave. The works of this thinker, Thumāmah Ibn al-Ashras, would possess some interest for us: he had the reputation of being a scoffer, and is said to have called those who flocked to the mosque cattle, wondering what "that Arab," viz. the Prophet, had made of them. A tradition also makes him obtain the execution of a man who charged the philosophers of his own school with heresy.

Of the numerous founders of schools who arose in the second and third centuries of Islam, only one, it appears, is known at first hand; voluminous as were the works of the others, they were not allowed to survive. The two main tendencies which sectarians followed—belief in the freedom of the will, and belief in justification by faith without works—were so unpopular with orthodox Moslems that books in which these opinions were defended had little chance of surviving. Traditions were invented, which are gravely cited by orthodox writers, in which the Prophet condemned the holders of both these opinions unsparingly; the Believers in the Freedom of the Will were called by him, it was said, "the Mazdians of this nation"; for by making man a free agent they established in nature a power outside God. He further asserted that the Murjis were accursed by the mouth of seventy prophets. Their name was then unknown; but the Prophet explained that he meant those who regarded faith as verbal expression only. Yet we fancy that the verbal expression was that to which he attached most importance—if there be any truth in his biography.

Still, numerous works have been preserved by one of these founders of sects—Jāḥiẓ of Baṣrah, probably the most important of all Moslem authors, whose treatises are mines of information on Arab antiquities and the civilisation of the Islam of the first centuries after the Migration. A certain amount of controversial matter is to be found in the most lengthy of his as yet published works—the zoology. It is curious that the same writer who charges Jāḥiẓ with having plagiarised his zoology from Aristotle also declares that Aristotle got his from the Arabs. Neither charge can be sustained: the amount which Jāḥiẓ owes to the Greek philosopher is very slight; he only cites Aristotle occasionally, and probably not at first hand, though he is aware that the Greek treatises have suffered much from clerical errors and mistranslation. In general he appears rather anxious to get away from his subject than to adhere to it, and the reader will certainly learn more from the digressions than from what is said on the supposed theme.

This work contains some reports of discussions between Moslems and Jews, Christians, or Mazdians, and these seem to have been conducted with good temper. Considerable curiosity seems in most ages to have been displayed by Moslems with regard to the doctrines of those sects which they permitted to exist, and it is likely that their representatives were more often the defending than the attacking party ; even where the Moslem bestows praise on members of these subject cults, he makes no secret of his claim of superiority. Still, in the process of discovering their doctrines and learning how they were defended the Moslem naturally had his attention drawn to his own system and what view it was supposed to hold on the subject ; and, as has been seen, the Koran had often to decide a question on which it either gave no answer or gave more than one.

From the statements in the zoology it would appear that various questions which are included in ontology and metaphysics had been greatly exercising the minds of the Moslem theologians, and the reconciliation of even elementary science with the Koran had not been found easy. If the stars and sun were not merely lamps, as the Koran asserted, but bodies, as the Greek astronomy taught, how could the former be flung at demons? Jāḥiz discusses this difficult matter, and replies that it need not necessarily apply to all the stars, but only to some; and since the stars are innumerable, it is absurd to suppose that any one would be missed from the sky if it were flung at a demon; and the Koran need not necessarily mean that the whole star was so flung, but may refer only to its flame.

The existence of the jinn themselves was not easy to reconcile with Greek science, and yet the Koran says too much about them to permit of their being simply rejected. Jāḥiz devotes a long section to proving their existence chiefly by the assertions of well-known persons who had come in contact with them. The stories here told seem excessively childish, *e.g.* accounts of unions between male jinn and women, or female jinn and men; a grandson of Iblis himself had lived and been known in Kufah. Whether consciously descending to the level of his audience, or himself entertaining these opinions, it

is certain that this founder of a freethinking sect
lends his name to the grossest superstitions.   He has
a chapter on the evil eye, which he endeavours to
explain, and of which he gives some notable examples ;
and he is also a believer in spells.   The Caliph Manṣūr,
wishing to test the powers of a snake-charmer, had
a leaden snake made and inserted in his roof : he
then summoned a charmer to deal with it   For a
long time this leaden model resisted the utmost
efforts of the charmer ; finally it melted—literally—
and came down from its perch.

The fragments of metaphysical discussions which
this book contains seem, then, only partially serious,
yet they are probably fair specimens of what went
on in the mosques where these matters were discussed.
The Koran has of course to be quoted at every stage ;
where it fails, recourse is had to tradition.

In the course of the discussions it became clear that
certain beliefs could only be held by the *dahriyyah*
" atheists," persons who denied the existence of
angels, jinn, prophets, witchcraft, and spells.   Such
an opinion was that of the eternity of matter ; clearly
matter, like everything else, was not eternal, but had
been created by God.

Attention has been called to this zoology because
outside it, in lieu of the works of the heretics, we
have selections from their doctrines made indeed
by an author of the early fifth century of Islam,
who appears to have possessed many of them and
to have studied them with care, but is himself
violently antagonistic and enumerates the dogmas

of these persons as so many disgraces. The range of subjects these lost works covered seems to have been as wide as that covered by the encyclopædias of the Greeks of old; these theologians had their own physical and metaphysical systems, and to a certain extent their logic, their ethics, and their systems of law. They are quoted for innovations in matters which come strictly within the domain of the jurist no less than for such as belong to theology. Nazzām is charged with having limited the amount which constituted a theft punishable with loss of the hand to 200 dirhems, whereas the great jurists settled that the punishment was to be incurred by a theft of $2\frac{1}{2}$ dirhems. He also denied that a divorce could be effected by any form of words other than that which expressed the husband's intention with absolute plainness. They also made incursions into the region called Principles of Jurisprudence. Abu'l-Hudhail demanded as evidence for a tradition no fewer than twenty witnesses, one of whom must be known to have been qualified for Paradise. To some extent the criticism of Moslem history came within their scope; they passed judgment on those early Moslem heroes and heroines who had taken part in civil wars.

Whether Islam gained or lost by these sectarian developments may be a subject of dispute; the charge that Islam was ruined by the introduction of Greek science and philosophy is in any case untenable, since, as has been seen, the questions were posed and the sects formed before Greek thought had reached the Moslems except in those results which had become common property. The formulation of Islamic dogma was as much a necessity due to the settlement of the Islamic empire as was the codification of the law; just as magistrates had to know what was the law in a variety of cases, so those who were constantly and perforce using the words "faith," "the soul," "God," "the next world," had to know what they ought to think about them. And since Islam was far more a political than a religious system, the opinions evolved could not easily be separated from Islamic politics, and in any classification of the sects political and metaphysical questions are hopelessly mixed. When Greek philosophy was actually pressed into the service, its results were at times accepted blindly, at times rejected fanatically. That the Islamic world awoke to the appreciation of these monuments before Western Europe seems to be attested, and some familiar phrases, like *premise* in logic, retain the memory of this. Yet that Islamic authors added nothing to Greek philosophy seems also to be attested, since when once Western Europe had recovered the Greek originals it discarded for good the Arabic intermediaries.

LECTURE VIII

IT is said that at the time of the French Revolution there were persons who wished to destroy all earlier literature so that the world might begin afresh. It would seem that such a view of the function and nature of Islam had impressed itself on the Prophet's imagination towards the end of his life, when he supposed that a new cosmic era had commenced. The relative positions of the planets had come back to the same as they had occupied at the beginning of creation. Whereas, then, Islam had at first been conceived of as based on earlier missions, which it continued and applied to the special needs of Arabia rather than superseded, when the idea of world-conquest had become connected with it, it could afford to reject that basis. The maxim " Islam cancels all that is before it," of the utmost importance in morals and law, also came to be historically applied. The amount of past history which the Koran contained was all that was worth knowing. Converts to Islam desired to forget their past: when asked questions about the earlier condition, they reply with the fixed formula, " God has put an end to all that, so why recur to it?" The process which we have seen to have been carried out in jurisprudence found its analogue in history: practice did not mean "uninterrupted practice," but the Prophet's practice; the era at which human memory commenced was the life of the Prophet, and only such practice as was sanctioned then had value or was to be maintained. Similarly, no preceding history had value; but that time, when men were living who saw and heard the Prophet, could not be sufficiently studied.

It is doubtless owing to this that Arabic authors have so little that is of value to record about Arabia. In South Arabia, where writing was so familiar and so long practised, it is difficult to believe that there were no written chronicles; and even in Central Arabia something was probably known about the origin and age of the most important cities. Yet it is the fact that with the Moslems real and continuous history commences with the Prophet's Migration; what precedes that date is a mass of fiction, wherein some facts may lie buried or occasionally appear. It can indeed be used in illustration of matter which happens to be known from some trustworthy source; but for other purposes it is worthless. Even of the pre-Islamic worships the Arabian archæologists have practically nothing to add to the meagre statements of the Koran; and the rule that no case may be judged simply by the statements of one litigant ought not to be discarded in this matter. We should like to know what the pagan priests and worshippers said or thought about their gods and goddesses as well as what the Koran says.

Those who ventured outside the Koran and consulted the books which the Koran ostensibly confirms found themselves confronted with a difficulty. It was quite true that Pharaoh, Korah, and Haman were mentioned in the Old Testament; but whereas in the Koran Haman is the vizier of the Egyptian king, in the Old Testament he is the minister of a Persian king who lived about a thousand years later; and whereas in the Koran, Korah—if he be meant by Ḳārūn—figures as a man of vast wealth who was punished for trusting to it, in the Old Testament there is nothing about this, and his punishment is for a very different offence. Now, in the Old Testament and its continuation in the New, the narratives hang together in chronological sequence, and the transference of Haman from the time after the Exile to that of Moses is unthinkable. Those, therefore, who consulted the books of the Jews and Christians found themselves plunged not into light but into darkness—on the assumption that the Koran was the infallible word of God and that it confirmed previous revelations.

According to the tradition, Mòhammed actually forbade his followers to read the books which the Koran ostensibly confirmed, alleging that the copies of the Jews and Christians had been intentionally corrupted: a charge which in the Koran itself is confined to the actual recitation; but he is also supposed in the case of serious discrepancies between his statements and those of the older sacred books to have harmonised them by some gentler method. Eventually there came to pass what might have been expected to happen; when the authority of the Koran was so secured that there was no danger of its being shaken, illustration and supplementing from the Jewish and Christian books were occasionally practised, though scarcely commended;[1] and indeed it is probable that certain converts from the older systems gladly used and even paraded their knowledge, which, so far as it served to illustrate the Koran, would be sure of appreciation. The citation of these works in confirmation of the Koran was thus permissible, but naturally they were not to be heard when they contradicted it.

To the rest of pagan history the Moslem attitude was not dissimilar to the modern European attitude with regard to far-off history: the man of ordinary education is not required to be familiar with the ancient Egyptian dynasties, or with the sequence of the Babylonian kings. What he usually knows about them is what is told either in the Bible or in Herodotus, not what has been made out from the inscriptions by specialists.

One method of dealing with the discrepancies between the Biblical narratives and the Koran was to supply the original Bible which the Jews and Christians had been supposed to corrupt. Copies of such works are occasionally found; they are close imitations in style of the Koran, and therefore take

1 Ibn Khallikān ii. 148.

the form of addresses by the Divine Being to the prophets to whom they are supposed to have been revealed. Apparently Sprenger was misled into supposing that a book of this kind, bearing the name of Abraham, was the Roll of Abraham to which some early Surahs of the Koran refer. The Ṣūfī Abū Ṭālib al-Mekkī makes tolerably frequent use of a collection which he calls "the Israelite traditions," some of which are evidently based on narratives actually found in the Bible. Thus he tells the story of the Temple of Jeroboam and the adventure of the prophet who announced its fall with very fair accuracy; proper names are indeed omitted, and the whole story is a sort of replica of the Mosque of *Ḍirār* or "nonconformity," which was built by some of the disaffected near the end of the Prophet's career, and of which the Prophet ordered the destruction; only the prophet who disobeyed the order is shown by a special revelation to have been eaten by the lion not as a punishment, but as an honour. One Khaithamah declared that the Gospel contained a statement about the keys of Korah's treasure-houses, which according to the Koran were a load for several persons; the Gospel gave the exact weight.[1] The "Gospel" perhaps was also responsible for a long story about the relations between Korah and Moses, in which the latter is credited with introducing a code identical with that of Mohammed. In these cases we have to do with pure fiction; but, as we have seen, at times the information really goes back

[1] Ṭabarī, Comm. xx. 63–68.

to the Jewish or Christian Scriptures, only it is altered in the interest of Islam. Abū Nu'aim gives a sort of epitome of the prophecies of Isaiah, wherein the Servant of the Lord is interpreted as the Prophet; some verses are quoted almost literally, but they are interpolated with other matter so as to bring in the chief facts of the Prophet's life. He also gives a fairly accurate account of the Vision of Nebuchadnezzar, only he naturally makes the stone cut out of the living rock to stand for the Mohammedan religion. The " Israelite traditions " were not merely repeated orally; Abū Ṭālib tells us that he had read in a Surah of the Torah called " the Surah of Yearning," how the Divine Being taunted someone with the interest which he took in a letter from a friend as compared with his neglect of the divine revelation and the messages which it contained. Yet we learn how little the actual books were consulted from the fact that such a scholar as Jāḥiẓ records stories which one of the early proselytes told out of the Torah on the authority of that proselyte, and merely *guesses* that by the Torah he means one of the other books to be found in the Jewish Bible.[1]

The theory that we should not differentiate between the prophets, which is a maxim of the Koran, and which perhaps accounts for a certain carelessness that we find in the New Testament as to the ascription of prophecies, leads to the attribution of sayings to personages who, we may be sure, never uttered them; thus there is a saying attributed

[1] Ḥayawān iv. 66.

to Christ to the effect that by saying the prescribed prayers a man escapes God's vengeance, and by prayers of supererogation wins his way to God's favour; but we are told that there was a similar saying ascribed to the Prophet Mohammed, to whom it is somewhat more appropriate. Where the older books are actually quoted, there is usually a tendency to expand or repeat, or at any rate introduce unnecessary verbiage, even where the sense is not seriously altered. A lengthy example is quoted in *Mohammedanism*;[1] another which may be given from the work of Abū Ṭālib al-Mekkī is that Christ said, "Sit not with the dead, lest your hearts die." He was asked, "Who are the dead?" He replied, "Those who love the world and desire it." That this is a reminiscence of a passage in the Gospel may be allowed; but it preserves more of the commentary than of the text. Similar paraphrases are to be found of passages of Isaiah, such as "This people approacheth me with the lips, but their heart is far from me"; though in this case the application is correct, or at least appears to be so. Occasionally the source of the references is some Jewish Midrash, either existing or lost. So we are told that Asaph committed some offence so terrible that it had best not be mentioned, but was pardoned; whereas the offence of Balaam was comparatively mild, but it was not pardoned.

These apocrypha, however, seem to have contained mainly homiletic matter, and possibly an occasional

---

[1] P. 207.

prophecy relating to the coming of the Prophet; indeed the Koran declares that the name Aḥmad is to be found in the Gospel, and an ancient charge against the Jews is that of having altered a description of the Prophet which was to be found in the Law. In consequence of these Biblical or pseudo-Biblical studies the Moslems became familiar with a few Old Testament names which are not found in the Koran; those of the New Testament at all times remained strange to them.

But if the records of the Jews and Christians had to be rewritten for edifying purposes, those of early Islam required something of the same sort. It is curious how little of the miraculous or the homiletic is found in the earliest life of the Prophet: its author Ibn Ishāḳ composed it in a form which required some expurgation at the hands of its earliest editors; the editor whose recension has come down to us confesses that he omitted matter calculated to give offence. Even so Ibn Ishāḳ places all the generosity, the heroism, and the public and private virtues on the side of Mohammed's enemies. The character which he gives the Companions of the Prophet is rarely pleasing, even if it is not actually repulsive. All these persons had somehow to be compelled to live up to their characters, and to be furnished besides with supplies of wise and noble sayings. The period of the pious Caliphs came to be depicted as a sort of halcyon days of the world, when the rulers set an example of piety and justice such as the world has never seen at any other time.

With regard to the life of the Prophet, the fictions wherewith it was embellished were rarely such as to impair the historical narrative. The order of events almost from the commencement of the mission was of such grave importance for a variety of reasons that serious alteration was not easily possible; the chronology of that career had come to be bound up with a variety of vested interests, whence it was not possible to disturb it. The hands and arms whereon the Prophet had relied were so well known, the exploits of the champions of Islam so celebrated, that they had to be admitted. In a letter which is some ten years earlier in date than the first biography of the Prophet, the Caliph Manṣūr assumes that the main facts of it are known: the genuineness of the letter is evinced by the fact that its author carelessly misquotes the Koran. The attempts that are made to whitewash the *heros eponymus* of the Abbasids, the Prophet's uncle ‘Abbās, by making him out a secret adherent of the Prophet, are either clumsy or unconvincing. History was not seriously affected by mild fictions, showing how the Prophet had decided various cases that had come up for decision, or attributing to him stores of wisdom on all subjects, not excepting medicine and cookery. The canon which we have seen to be assumed or formulated, that the Prophet's practices should be preferred to the product of the reasoning faculty, was a safeguard against serious misrepresentation of his career; for since a thing was right because he had said or done it, his character would not suffer from anything that might be recorded about him. Still, it could not be expected that his followers would wish otherwise than that his character should be regarded as admirable by any standard; and in treatises of metaphysical theology the unapproachable perfection of the Prophet's character is urged as a proof of his mission.

On the other hand, there is a principle deeply grounded in human nature that such claims as were made by the Prophet, and maintained by him and his adherents on his behalf at the sword's point, should be backed by something more overwhelming than perfections of character, of style, or even of scholarship. The miracle of the Koran, which consists in the unattainable perfections of the latter, was not sufficient for ages in which a high standard of correctness and even of eloquence was demanded of all writers, and wherein the historical matters to which the Koran makes allusion were matters of common knowledge. It was probably difficult to realise the degree of ignorance wherewith the Prophet credits himself and his Meccan contemporaries; and the Koran itself credited certain prophets, notably Moses and Jesus, with performances to which the plain biography of Mohammed offered no parallel. When Moslems consented to argue with Jews or Christians, grave embarrassment must have been occasioned by this proof of superiority which the opponents could adduce from the irrefragable testimony of the Moslem Scriptures. Hence a not unnatural endeavour was made to meet these opponents on their own ground:

to accept the natural opinion that a supernatural mission must be attested by supernatural powers; but to show that the exploits of the Islamic Prophet in this field fell short in no way of those which had formed the glory of the founders of Judaism and Christianity.

The miracle whereby history was least falsified was prophecy: Mohammed could be credited harmlessly with having foretold the most noteworthy events of the period which followed his death. Thus he foretold how and when Ali should die; he warned Zubair that he would fight against Ali, but that he would be in the wrong; he warned his wife 'Ā'ishah that at one of his wives the dogs of Ḥau'ab would bark, and that this would be the worse for her; and 'A'ishah recalled this saying on her way to stir up the people of Baṣrah against Ali—the commencement of that civil war which never really stopped. When another eminent follower of the Prophet, 'Ammār Ibn Yāsir, was slain on the field of Ṣiffīn, it was remembered how the Prophet had foretold that he would be killed by usurpers, and indeed uttered this prophecy at the time when the Mosque of Medinah was being built. We have already seen him credited with prophecies about the chief sects of Islam, whose names had not been invented in his lifetime. These inventions naturally led to some difficulties, which it required some further exercise of the imagination to solve. If 'A'ishah had really been warned about the dogs of Ḥau'ab, how came she to continue her expedition? If Ali knew who was to be his assassin, why did he not anticipate the blow? If Zubair had been told beforehand that he would be in the wrong in his dispute with Ali, why did he persist therein? Even in the case of Fāṭimah, who was told by the dying Prophet that she was to follow him speedily, it was clear that the prophecy had no influence either on her conduct or that of anyone else.

A considerable collection of matter, with the usual chains of authorities, attesting the miraculous elements in the Prophet's career, was put together in the fourth century of Islam by one Abū Nu'aim, under the title "Proofs of the Prophetic Mission." Any reader of hagiologies is aware that the human fancy is ordinarily somewhat sterile, and the circumstances of a miraculous career admit of only slight variations. The fancy is by no means satisfied with such a career commencing late in life; Mohammed must have been a prophet from his birth—nay before his birth—nay from the beginning of the world. The second chapter of the *Dalā'il* gives evidence showing that the Prophet's call took place when Adam was half created, when his clay had been modelled but the spirit had not yet been infused. The statement, indeed, goes back to the Prophet himself; but some external attestation is also adduced. When the Prophet first announced his mission in Meccah, a certain Jubair Ibn Muṭ'im went on a trading expedition to Bosra; there some Christians assured him that in a collection of statues they had one of the Prophet who was to come forth, and requested him to see whether he

16

could identify the statue of Mohammed. He could not find it in the first monastery into which he was taken, but found it easily in the second. This collection of prophetic statues fortunately served to settle another controversy, viz. that between the two great sects of Islam ; for this monastery contained not only the image of the Prophet, but also that of his legitimate successor, who turned out to be Abū Bakr.

Another anecdote of the same sort follows, but it is less convincing, since it is located after the Prophet's death, when a mission was sent by Abū Bakr to the Byzantine sovereign who happened to be in Damascus. He exhibits to his visitors a whole collection of portraits on silk,. among which they recognise that of their Prophet ; the rest, as the king explains, are representations of his pre-decessors, beginning with Adam. To the question whence the king had got this valuable collection of portraits he replied that Adam had requested to be shown the figures of all his prophetic posterity, and this request had been granted by Allah; they remained in the Treasury of Adam in the West till it was plundered by Alexander the Great. At some time Daniel obtained access to them and copied them, and apparently Daniel's copies were those shown in Damascus. What the collection proved was that the Prophet's call was at the least coeval with the creation of Adam.

Neither of these stories is free from religious objections ; for since statues are tabooed, and pictures

disapproved by the pious, neither of these impro-
prieties ought to be associated with the Prophet.
On the other hand, Christianity dealt so much in
icons of religious personages that Mohammed might
reasonably be expected to be found somewhere in
the company of those with whom the Koran regularly
associates him. The story of the pictures on silk
seems also to bear some relation to the Veronica
napkin.

If we consider how orthodox Islam denies the
credibility of Jews or Christians, we may feel some
surprise at the anxiety with which attestations of
these sectarians to the genuineness of the Prophet's
mission are got together. Immediately before the
Prophet's arrival at Medinah a Jew there named
Joshua foretold that such a personage would come
thither from Meccah during the lifetime of some then
present; unfortunately this harbinger of the Prophet
himself refused to believe in the mission which he
had foretold—a circumstance which seems to have
occurred at other times. When the Prophet's court-
poet Ḥassān Ibn Thābit was seven or eight years
of age, a Jew of the Ḳoraiẓah tribe standing on the
top of his fortress announced to the other Jews the
rising of the Prophet Aḥmad's star; which also
portended destruction to their countrymen in Arabia.
It is rather interesting that by this time the Jews
should be sufficiently associated with astrology to
be able of themselves to discharge the task for which
the Magi are called in in the Christian Gospel.
Indeed the coming of Aḥmad and his figure were

so well known to the Medinese Jews before the Prophet's call that the children used to be taught all about him in the schools. Some dissentient Arabs after the Prophet had become powerful went to seek the aid of the Egyptian governor, whom the Arabs call Muḳauḳis—a puzzling expression, which has not yet been interpreted with certainty; to their astonishment, the Muḳauḳis argued forcibly in favour of the Prophet's veracity, and the inquiries addressed to bishops of the Alexandrian communities with reference to the description of Mohammed to be found in the Christian books were so satisfactorily answered that these Arabs were converted. Some of the invaders of Irak came across a cave in which there lived one Darīb, son of Bartholomew, who had remained alive since the time of Jesus; he sent warm greetings to Omar with a confession of faith in Mohammed.

We find that among the confessors to whose testimony some weight is attached in the Gospels are demons, even when they are driven out. The Prophet's relations with these beings were on the whole friendly, and we learn from the Koran that a number of them adopted Islam; but it was desirable to get some of their testimony recorded by others than the Prophet himself. The first harbinger of the mission at Medinah was a pagan woman visited by a spirit which took the form of a white bird perched on a wall; when the woman asked it to converse, it replied that a prophet had now arisen in Meccah who had told the jinn to quit. A sorceress consulted

by Othman in Syria was told by her familiar that
he could now no longer enter her door, because
Aḥmad had appeared and the jinn had to make
themselves scarce. Other sorcerers in Arabia were
warned by their familiars that their trade was now
abolished, since they had now no chance of eaves-
dropping at the heavenly council-chamber. An idol
in Samāya, a village of Oman, found voice one day
at a sacrifice and bade the sacrificers follow the
religion of Aḥmad who had just appeared. It seems
rather hard on this idol that the sacrificer in answer
to this message destroyed it. On the other hand, the
priest obtained through the Prophet's intercession a
variety of blessings, including four wives. Voices
were heard from the interior of other fetishes calling
on their worshippers to abandon idolatry and follow
the true faith. It is conceivable that some of these
tales may go back to the time of the Prophet, when
the Arab chieftains were hurrying to pay homage to
the new ruler and excogitating ingenious flatteries.
The most popular of all is the romance of the wizard
Saṭīḥ, a creature without bones or sinews, who could
be folded up like a garment ; and who, imitating the
exploit of Daniel, repeated to a Ghassanide king a
dream which he had seen, foretelling the fortunes of
Arabia and the arrival of the Prophet.

That the Prophet's nativity should be graced with
miracles was to be expected, though we have here
a difficulty which is found in other cases: such
miraculous antecedents ought, one fancies, to have
prepared the people of Meccah for the mission when

it came, whereas historically they appear to have been wholly unprepared for it. The women who attended Āminah, the Prophet's mother, at her confinement saw the stars fall and heard mysterious voices; the mother of one of the foremost Companions, named Shifā, was one of these, and she treasured up these experiences until the call came. That the powers of evil should make some attempt to kill him in his youth was also to be expected; when he was being reared as an infant among the Banu Sa'd a sorcerer endeavoured to bring about his death, but his nurse succeeded in rescuing him. It is rather strange that no such attempt seems to be recorded on the part of the Persian king, who was warned of the Prophet's birth by a whole series of portents, including the fall of a portion of his palace and the extinction of the sacred fire " which had not been extinguished for a thousand years "; he so far plays the part of Herod that he solicits the aid of magicians in interpreting these prodigies; but though he learns that they portend trouble to come from the direction of Arabia, he does not appear to have taken any step to anticipate it. Like Hezekiah he seems to have been satisfied with a promise that the trouble should not come in his time.

Edifying fiction of this sort has to hover between two contradictory assumptions—one that the infant is highly esteemed, the other that he belonged to the humblest class; thus we are told that Mohammed's clan was so wealthy, and his arrival so welcome, that the whole population of Meccah was entertained lavishly by his grandfather on the occasion of his birth ; on the other hand, that none of the wet-nurses who came to Meccah to find employment would look at Mohammed, because they could not expect to gain by nursing a fatherless boy. Hence he had to be taken by a woman who had failed to secure any foster-child, and the woman prospered marvellously in consequence.

It was to be expected that the migration to Medinah should somehow be anticipated, and so Mohammed is made to go to Medinah in his sixth year, being taken thither by his mother on a visit to her relations. Some of the Jews visit the house where he lodges with his mother, and are allowed to investigate his person, where they search for the signs of prophecy. These, of course, they find, and inform his relations that they have with them the Prophet of the Arabs, who will one day migrate to their city, where he will massacre the Jews. A slave-girl who goes with them "treasures these things in her heart."

The imagination is not much exercised over the years which he is said to have spent under the guardianship of his grandfather and his uncle ; the persons who are made to foretell his greatness are, as before, Jews and Christians, because it is clear that the Arabs have no expectation of a Prophet or Messiah. One member of a tribe which practised tracking does indeed notice the extraordinary resemblance of the Prophet's foot to that of Abraham, whose sole had left its imprint on a stone in the Meccan sanctuary. At the meals, necessarily scanty, provided by Abū Ṭālib for his household, it was observed that if the Prophet were present there was always enough and to spare; if he were absent, no one had enough.

In spite of his appointment to the prophetic office having been made when Adam was only half created, some further consecration was required; and this was by a baptism of the heart, two angels splitting his stomach and washing the contents with snow before replacing them. The angels appeared in the form of white birds to a playmate of the Prophet, but he does not seem to have witnessed the rest of the scene. We have already seen that " purity of heart " is interpreted literally by the Moslem mystics, as a state to be produced by fasting, whence there is nothing incongruous about this material purgation. The story looks like a conscious improvement on that of the Saviour's baptism, especially in the introduction of the angels in the form of birds; it was argued that an internal cleansing rather than an external was requisite. Further, Arabia, and especially Meccah, has no river which could serve as the analogue of the Jordan. The word " clean " is that which Arabic theologians employ for " holy "; and in the Koran the Prophet is bidden clean his garments, where garments, it is supposed, may stand for " heart." That the heart of man is the source of defilement is taught in the Gospel, in a striking passage which was doubtless familiar to many who were but slightly acquainted with the Gospel. The pious inventor of this story, then, wished to devise a scheme whereby in the Prophet's case this source of pollution should have been rendered clean, and though his method is somewhat naïve, it was effective. The phrase " washing with snow " is probably due to a slight confusion of thought, its author meaning washing snow-white.

In the narrative of the Prophet's journey with the caravan to Syria we leave the area of the New Testament and get traits from the historical books of the Old Testament. The monk Baḥīrā of Bosra notices that as the caravan proceeds a cloud rests on the head of Mohammed, and when they alight under a tree, the cloud overshadows the tree, which becomes covered with green leaves. Though he has previously shown the traders no hospitality, he on this occasion arranges a banquet to which he invites the whole caravan with an urgent request that no one should stay away. Naturally the Prophet, as the youngest of the party, does not suppose himself to be included in the invitation. Baḥīrā, however, notices that the cloud is over the head of none among the company, and demands that the young absentee be sent for ; Mohammed comes, and is followed by the cloud, whereas the tree under which he had taken shelter pulls itself up by the roots. He adjures Mohammed by the idols Lāt and ʿUzzā to answer certain questions, which the Prophet willingly answers, but declares that he has abjured Lāt and ʿUzzā. Some Jews endeavour to enlist Baḥīrā in a conspiracy against the life of Mohammed, but the monk ensures his safety.

The only detail in this narrative that is not based on the history of Moses and of David seems to be that of the tree, which figures rather more significantly in the story of the second expedition, where the monk who receives them bears the name Nestorius. The Prophet takes shelter under a tree; and the monk states that his doing so is a clear sign of prophecy; only prophets take shelter under that particular tree. The tree appears to be a reminiscence of the fig-tree in the first chapter of St John, where, however, it is the convert Nathanael who is seen under the fig-tree.

Mohammed enters history as the leader of a caravan carrying the merchandise of the wealthy Khadījah; when Khadījah learns that Mohammed is willing to discharge this service, she offers him twice the fee which she would have given to anyone else. This is a fiction somewhat in the style of Josephus, merely intended to lend the transaction additional dignity.

Every one of these stories is preceded by its chain of authorities, and made to rest ultimately on the assertion of someone who had good opportunities of knowing the truth; and Abū Nu'aim, concluding this collection of anecdotes dealing with the Prophet's youth and infancy, argues that the miraculous elements which they contain are sufficient to attest the truth of the Prophet's mission, especially if we take into account the fact that he was identified by persons who were in possession of a description, and were on the look-out for an individual answering to it. The Messiah whom they were expecting was to have a permanent redness in the eye—-a characteristic of Judah in the Blessing of Jacob, though there ascribed to the effect of wine-drinking—a weal between his shoulder-blades, and certain other peculiarities, such as are put by the police into the hands of detectives; they detected the Prophet by these marks. Only, as appears to be regularly the case with oracles, people completely forgot that they had ever been given until after they had been fulfilled. Nor does the conduct of any contemporary of the Prophet appear to have been at all influenced by the phenomena which accompanied his presence.

It was obviously undesirable that the Prophet should at any time of his life have been an idolator, and, as we have seen, quite early in his career he is made to repudiate all connection with the Meccan goddesses. It was, however, a question how he could have lived in Meccah for some forty years and kept aloof from the worships of his countrymen. Since all feasts were idolatrous services, he had to be kept away from them, and indeed by supernatural means. When it was his turn to touch an idol, he felt a tall man in white garments intervene and tell him to go back. At other times when he felt an inclination to do as the people of Meccah, he was miraculously sent to sleep.

There does not appear to be in these legends any exact parallel to the Gospel narrative of the Temptation, but there are some analogues. When the Prophet was prostrating himself in Meccah, Satan wished to tread upon his neck; Gabriel arrived in time to blow Satan away, and indeed as far as the Jordan. A more serious raid upon him was made by a troop of demons, Satan himself bearing a torch, with which he intended to burn the Prophet; this time Gabriel taught him a spell which drove the horde away. Mohammed had indeed, like every other human being, a demon attached to him; he was, however, able to convert this inconvenient parasite, and reduce him to submission.

In the historical account of the Prophet's flight from Meccah, he escapes the attempt on his life by a mixture of cunning, resolution, and daring. This method might not seem good enough, and therefore something more worthy of the Prophet of God was devised. When he is informed that the Meccans have conspired together to kill him as soon as they see him, he comes forward boldly; their eyes droop and their hands are powerless; he flings a handful of pebbles at them, and all on whom those pebbles fall are afterwards slain at Badr. Various other people attempt his life, among them the notorious Abū Jahl, but are miraculously prevented from carrying out their intentions; they seize stones, which stick to their hands, or else their hands wither in the style of Jeroboam's. Like Jeroboam they have to implore the Prophet's intercession before they can recover the use of their fingers. And lest Balaam should be favoured with a miracle denied the Prophet, an animal is made to talk for his benefit. When the Prophet came back from Badr victorious, a Jewess met him with a roast kid, which she said she had vowed to slaughter in the event of his coming back from the expedition with triumph; but the kid rose up on its four legs and said to the Prophet, " Eat me not, I am poisoned ! "

In the Koran itself the Prophet is made to disclaim miracles on various grounds, chiefly their ineffectiveness in producing belief among the stiffnecked. Nevertheless it would be more satisfactory if the demand had been satisfied, and the historical supplement satisfies it amply. Like Hezekiah the Meccans demand a sign in heaven, viz. the splitting of the full moon and its halves appearing on two different hills respectively. This actually happens in the presence of the leading Meccans, though there is some discrepancy as to the date. The Meccans declare it to be sorcery, *i.e.* what we should call an optical illusion, and wish to know whether anyone outside Meccah has seen the phenomenon; the next day it is confirmed by numerous travellers who arrive. There is indeed a reference to the splitting of the moon in the Koran, which appears to be one of the terrors which will accompany the Day of Judgment; and though this text is probably the basis of the story, the narrators were probably also moved by the desire to show that the Prophet could do as much or more than Joshua and Isaiah.

The Flight, or rather Migration, was the occasion of numerous miracles—two doves nested at the mouth of the cave in which the Prophet and his companion had taken refuge, and a spider took the opportunity to spin its web in the same place. Although, then, professional trackers found their way to this place of concealment, they were convinced that the cave had not been entered. At one point they were nearly overtaken by a pursuer on horseback; but ere he could reach them the horse's legs sank down deep in the hard rock. The pursuer was rescued from this perilous plight by the Prophet on condition that he put the other pursuers off the scent. The refugees alighted at a tent, where they asked for milk; there was only an emaciated ewe there, but the Prophet prayed, and it produced copious milk.

Of the miracles supposed to be performed by the Prophet during his residence at Medinah many took the form of healing, effected by his prayers. Thus a dumb child was brought him; he took water, used it for ablutions, and then gave it to the child's mother, who used it both as a lotion and a draught; by the end of a year the child could not only speak, but displayed extraordinary intelligence. On a journey he met a woman with a child who was subject to fits; the Prophet spat into the child's mouth, and told the devil in possession of the child to be quiet; on the return journey they met the mother and child in the same place, and were informed that the fits had not recurred. An even closer parallel to a New Testament miracle is told of a child possessed of a devil; the Prophet stroked its chest, whereupon the child vomited, and the demon came out in the shape of a black cub. A man who had lost his sight by treading upon snake's eggs applied to the Prophet for a cure ; this was effected with spittle, and was so perfect that the man at the age of eighty could thread his own needles.

Of miraculous supplies of food we have already had some examples ; there are others which imitate the precision of detail given in the Gospel miracle of the loaves and fishes. The great traditionalist Abū Hurairah was asked by the Prophet, apparently on a journey, whether he had any food ; he replied that he had some dates, to the number of twenty-seven, in a wallet. The Prophet bade him lay them out ; they furnished a copious meal to the company, and when all had been satisfied Abū Hurairah was told to count the leavings, restore them to the wallet, and whenever he wanted a date to put in his hand, but by no means to empty out the wallet. Abū Hurairah followed these instructions, and the dates lasted till twenty-six years after the Prophet's death, when they were stolen during the siege of Othman's palace. In this narrative the Gospel miracle has been combined with Elijah's of the widow's cruse. A somewhat closer parallel to the latter is recorded of the expedition to Tabuk ; the oil vessel was nearly empty, when its keeper fell asleep ; he woke to hear it bubbling in the sun, and put the cover on. Had he left it alone, said the Prophet, the whole valley would have been flowing with oil.

Abū Hurairah was also the witness of an occasion on which a single cup of milk served to satisfy all the people of the *Ṣuffah* or mendicant Moslems who had no home save the Mosque of Medinah. Other occasions were recorded whereon the Prophet miraculously increased supplies of water in the desert.

That the tradition records apparently no occasions whereon the Prophet raised the dead is worthy of notice, for this would seem to be the crowning miracle which ought not to have been omitted in the list of his exploits. Although logic enters very slightly into edifying fabrication of the sort with which we are dealing, there may have been strong theological reasons for abstaining from invention of this style. The martyrs of the Holy War were seen by the Prophet in Paradise, winged and happy; they sent messages by him expressing their satisfaction with their experiences, and it would be evidently hard on them that they should be brought back from the Garden of Delights. Further, it was not claimed for the Prophet himself that he rose from the dead, and if such resurrection were a privilege, it was unthinkable that it should have been accorded to others and denied him. Besides this, the Moslem tradition deals almost, though not quite exclusively, with historical personages: people who have parents and children, who can be located in various ways, and brought into connection with various other historical personages. The Prophet could not well be made to restore any of these to life; on the other hand, had he exercised this power at all, he could not well have failed to practise it on such heroes as Ḥamzah, or his own son Ibrahim. Hence the miracle-mongers have wisely kept to incidents which did not really affect the course of history; for no one could say how often the people of the Ṣuffah had to go without dinner or whence in any particular case they had procured it, nor did the Prophet's commissariat department keep any record of supplies and expenditure during the campaigns. The belief that hosts of angels fought on his side was wisely encouraged by the Prophet; for while it added glory to his victories it minimised the disgrace of the defeated; but it is clear that he never counted on the aid of these angels for any actual fighting, and he was probably far too cautious to attempt any miracle where failure might prove compromising. What we learn from the *Dalā'il al-Nubuwwah* is, then, nothing that is of value for the biography of the Prophet, but the effect which familiarity with Jews and Christians had perforce on the idea of a prophet as conceived by Moslem minds. Similarly, when the Moslems, owing to Arabic translations of the Bible, had learned the nature of the Old and New Testaments, they strove to show that the Koran in its different parts contained the analogue of the various parts of the older Scriptures: one part corresponded with the Law, another with the Psalms, another with the Gospel. Somewhat similarly, the Jewish Moses of renaissance times derives many a trait from the Prophet Mohammed; and when a few years ago a Jesuit writer on rhetoric in Arabic quoted Almighty God for rhetorical figures, he was certainly under the influence of his Moslem environment; the degree of sanctity assigned the Bible by a Christian ought not to fall short of that which the Mohammedan assigns the Koran. If a prophet and Messiah was a miracle-worker, and this was attested for the Christian Messiah by the Koran itself, the seal of the prophets ought clearly to be able to show as lengthy and striking a record in this matter as the greatest of his predecessors; and, as we have seen, that has on the whole been made out. If Mohammed fell short on any one point, he compensated for it by the number and importance of his other exploits.

In the development of a religion fiction has scarcely less importance than fact. In order to understand the rise of Islam it is necessary to be acquainted with the historical Mohammed—the man of extreme caution and extreme intrepidity: who made by force his merit known: who gauged with exactitude the intellect and the character of his associates and his adversaries; for whom every fortress had its key and every man his price: whom no opportunity escaped, no scruple deterred, and no emergency found unprepared. But for the continuance and development of the system probably the fictitious Mohammed was the more significant: the legislator, the saint, and the thaumaturge.

INDEX

* 9 7 8 1 9 3 1 5 4 1 9 4 7 *